YOUR BEST
RETIREMENT PLAN

YOUR BEST RETIREMENT PLAN

HOW TO ELIMINATE MARKET RISK, AVOID TAXES AND HAVE MONEY FOR THE REST OF YOUR LIFE

BILL KANTER, J.D., MBA

ISBN: 0692584684
ISBN-13: 978-0692584682

Disclaimer: This book is not intended to give any tax, financial or investment advice of any kind. The contents and materials and ideas in this book represent the opinions of the author and may not be applicable to all situations. The author hereby disclaims all warranties including without limitation warranties of fitness for a particular purpose. Please seek the advice of competent professionals before implementing any of the ideas in this work. The author assumes no responsibility for actions taken by readers based on the advice contained herein.

Expert Press
www.ExpertPress.net

This book is dedicated to
the memory of my dear father,

Rabbi Dr. Albert Milton Kanter.

"For I have loved him, because he commands his children and his household after him that they keep the way of God, doing charity and justice, in order that God might then bring upon Abraham that which he had spoken of him" (Genesis 18:19)

Contents

Acknowledgments

For Valerie, Daniel,
Aviva, Shimon,
Leah and Yonah.
Everything I do is for you.

OH, OH.. LOOKS LIKE OUR 401K IS NOW A 201K.

Introduction

Two True Stories And Two Powerful Questions

Joe

Joe came to one of my estate- and financial-planning seminars in October 2008. He was 72 years old, he had just retired and he was quite talkative. He asked questions during the seminar and complimented me on my presentation.

Because I had been discussing the concept of "safe money," the idea that in retirement one should not lose any money in the stock market, Joe came in to see me for an appointment. The stock market was tanking. By the time his appointment rolled around, it was November 2008 and he was quite unhappy and concerned. It was then that I first heard the expression, "My 401(k) is now a 201(k)." In Joe's case this was pretty accurate because his 401(k) statement, which just several months prior had shown a balance of over $400,000, was now sitting at approximately $275,000. This was quite a blow to Joe and his wife, who were trying to live for the rest of their lives off their Social Security income and his 401(k) plan.

Unfortunately, there was little I could do for Joe because he was drawing out his 401(k) money to live on and had no time to let it grow safely. To add insult to injury, the money that Joe was now drawing out of his plan was going to be taxed as ordinary income, which will further deplete the money he has to live on.

Joe is now 76 years old and back at work. I recently saw him at the job he has had for the last four years at Wal-Mart.

Fred

Fred is a bank manager. One day in 2014, while I was in the bank signing over a savings account to my newly 18-year-old son, I started talking to him.

When Fred found out I was a financial planner, he told me that he would have been four years into his retirement were it not for the crash of 2008. The crash cost Fred half the 401(k) money he had invested in mutual funds, forcing him to move what was left out to cash and etching 2010 into his memory not for being the year he retired as planned but for being the year he did not. It also affected some of Fred's friends and colleagues, managers and executives with whom he had gone to school, gotten started in banking and figured to retire.

But other colleagues, bankers who had gotten into the business a couple years earlier, had retired on schedule, in 2006.

Last I saw him, Fred still hadn't gotten back into the market. He was scared to do so. Who can blame him? The market's a moody beast, either up or down all the time. Besides the crashes that happen every six to eight years, there are smaller, more frequent downturns called corrections that occur every 18 months or so.

And yet though the market is cyclical, it's anything but predictable. In the famous *Wall Street Journal* dartboard contest, blindfolded WSJ staffers threw darts at a big board with stocks on it and compared the ones they hit with stocks picked by expert money managers. The stocks hit by darts often fared better.

Nobody outsmarts the stock market. So people who say they'll move their money into something more secure as they approach retirement are taking a big risk. Most individual investors lack the time and ability to consistently watch and understand what their funds are doing, and that puts them at a huge disadvantage. Why? I'll tell you why: A 401(k) plan is not the average investor's friend.

In their book *The Great 401(k) Hoax,* in fact, William Wolman and Anne Colamosca write that the 401(k) will turn out to be the greatest systematic financial hoax ever perpetrated on an unsuspecting public. Saving for retirement with a 401(k) or an IRA isn't merely a long road; it's also a hard one, fraught with white-knuckle hills and valleys, bone-jarring potholes and breathtaking blind curves. Not only will you endure the ups and downs and uncertainties of the market, you'll also:

- Turn your money over to a stranger—some guy or gal who puts together a basket of stocks and says, I'm part of Vanguard or Fidelity and I'm going to manage your money;
- Agree to defer all the taxes on your money to a future time when taxes might be higher and your deductions might be lower and you may have less income to pay the tax bill;

- Pay lots of hidden fees and other expenses that you don't even know you're paying and get absolutely nothing for in return; and
- Lash your fortunes to the twists and turns of faraway situations beyond your control—terrorist attacks or oil embargos or dot-com bubbles bursting or big banks going bust; the events that cause people to start selling off and the markets to crash.

If you think any of this sounds unwise, I agree.

Fortunately, there are better ways to save for retirement, ways that won't subject you to so much worry, surprise and loss.

In fact, there's absolutely no reason why having financial peace of mind tomorrow should preclude having it today.

This brings me to two questions with which I would like to begin this book:

1) Do you want to risk a catastrophic market downturn and loss in your IRA/401(k) and other retirement accounts in the years immediately preceding or during your retirement?
2) Would you like to have your retirement income entirely tax free and not just tax deferred like a traditional 401(k) or IRA?

The first question above will have more meaning after we look at the chart and graph on the next page. However, before going there consider the following three statements:

- *"The average 401(k) runs out of money 7 to 8 years into retirement."*—The Employee Benefit Research Institute

- *"The 401(k) plans...were never designed to be retirement plans in the first place...the big beneficiaries were the mutual funds."*—60 Minutes (hosted by Steve Kroft).
- *"Unless we begin to get our fiscal house in order, there's simply no other way to handle our ever-mounting debt burdens except by doubling taxes over time."*—David M. Walker, Former Comptroller General of the United States and Head of the Government Accountability Office.

Performance of $100,000 in an S&P 500 Index fund from Jan. 1, 1999 to Dec. 31, 2012 (Not including fees or taxes or possible dividends reinvested)

YEAR	Actual S&P 500 Performance Jan 1-Dec 31	S&P 500 Account Value
1999	19.51%	$119,500
2000	-10.14%	$107,383
2001	-13.04%	$93,380
2002	-23.37%	$71,557
2003	26.38%	$90,434
2004	8.99%	$98,564
2005	3.00%	$101,521
2006	13.62%	$115,348
2007	3.53%	$119,420
2008	-38.50%	$73,443
2009	23.45%	$90,665
2010	12.80%	$102,270
2011	00.00%	$102,270
2012	10.20%	$112,702
14 Year Total	0.86%	$112,702

Please keep the above chart in mind.
We will refer to it again in this book.

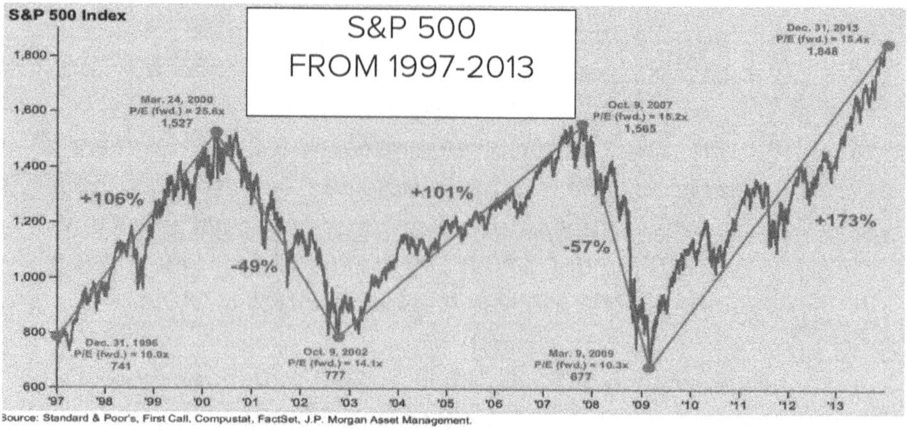

Source: Standard & Poor's, First Call, Compustat, FactSet, J.P. Morgan Asset Management.

What if you had planned to retire in 2002 or 2008 (like Fred the bank manager)?

Do you want to risk this scenario for <u>your</u> retirement?

<u>Bear Market Losses Since 1968</u>

November 29, 1968 to May 26, 1970	**-36.06%**
January 11,1973 to October 3, 1974	**-48.20%**
November 28, 1980 to August 12, 1982	**-27.11%**
August 25, 1987 to December 4, 1987	**-33.54%**
March 27, 2000 to July 18, 2002	**-42.29%**
October 9, 2007 to March 9, 2009	**-56.77%**

CAGLECARTOONS.COM
©2011 FLORIDA TODAY
NOT A GOOD SIGN. OUR STOCK BROKER ENCLOSED A MOTION SICKNESS BAG WITH OUR LATEST STATEMENT...
STOCK MARKET IN FOR A WILD RIDE AFTER U.S. CREDIT DOWNGRADE

Chapter 1

How We Got Into this Mess

After the stock market crash of 1929 eviscerated a great deal of wealth in this country, Congress realized that American workers were not saving enough and needed to supplement their personal retirement savings. On August 14, 1935, President Franklin D. Roosevelt signed the Social Security Act (SSA) into law. The SSA was set up only to ensure that retirees had basic living necessities during their retirement years. Social Security was never intended to be a person's sole source of retirement funds.

Corporations were also contributing to pension plans on behalf of their workers, and individuals were encouraged to save for their own retirement. For decades this "three-legged stool" was the cornerstone of retirement planning in this country.

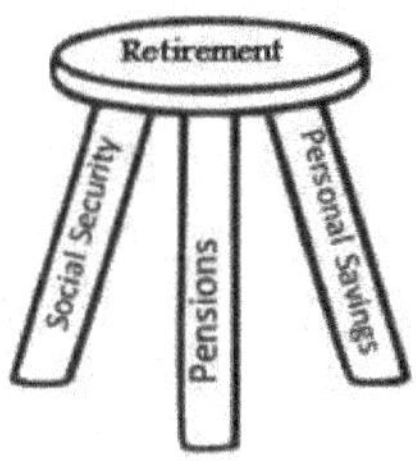

A great deal of the personal savings component of retirement planning was held in whole life insurance. The combination of tax-free growth and guaranteed dividends plus no stock market risk (people still remembered the crash of 1929), made cash-value life insurance a popular item.

> *"For decades, whole life, with its tax-free investment component, was the cornerstone of many families' security. The percentage of families buying such policies began sliding in the 1980s with the proliferation of other savings options such as mutual funds and 401(k) accounts."*
>
> —*Wall Street Journal,* October 3, 2010.

This all began to change in 1974, when Congress passed The Employee Retirement Income Securities Act (ERISA). Out of this act grew IRAs, 401(k) and other company-sponsored plans, SEPs, and 403(*b*) plans. ERISA was designed to encourage Americans to prepare for retirement and be less dependent on Uncle Sam.

More specifically, section 401(k) was part of the 1978 Internal Revenue Service Code. This section allowed for a "deferred arrangement" with annual contributions limited (currently to $17,500). The idea was that company executives with extra money could contribute to a tax-deferred retirement plan under this section. The 401(k) was never meant to be a primary retirement vehicle.

This all changed in 1980 when a benefits consultant named Ted Benna realized that this previously obscure provision of the code could be used to create a tax-advantaged way to save for retirement.

It is interesting to note that on November 23, 2011, *MSN Money* ran an article titled "Father of 401(k)' disowns it." In the article, they quote Benna saying that while he is proud to be known as the father of the 401(k), "I would blow up the system and restart with something totally different."

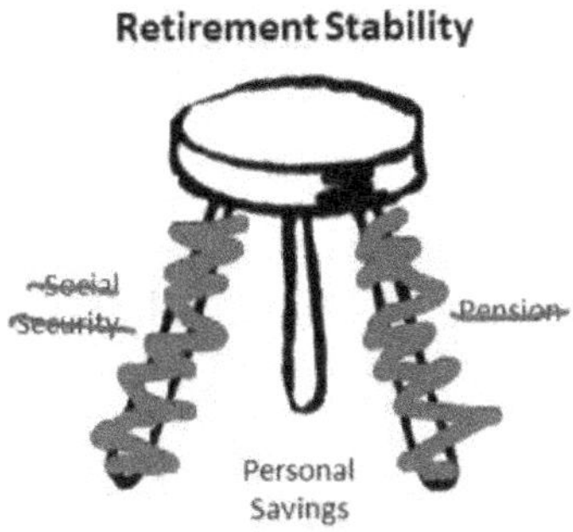

"The three-legged stool has gone to two legs and it's wobbly and I'm not sure it's going to support anything."

—Brooks Hamilton, consultant to the employee benefits industry, *60 Minutes*, April 19, 2009.

Hamilton pointed out that 401(k) plans became much cheaper for the employer to both manage and fund, because employer 401(k) matching contributions were much smaller than company pension plan contributions. As a result many companies did away with their pension plans. Wall Street sold this concept to corporate America. This created an enormous source of funds for Wall Street and the mutual fund industry, which pounced on the opportunity to manage the new retirement vehicle known as the 401(k). Millions of new "employee investors" now had their nest eggs on Wall Street.

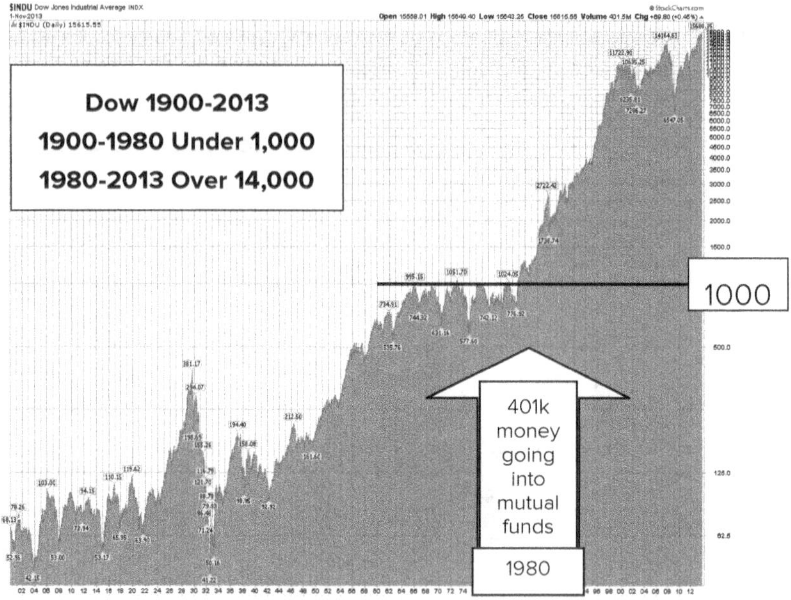

"If you go back and track the mutual fund growth in assets and you track the growth in 401(k) plans, it looks like a railroad track leading to the sky. They are parallel tracks. So the big beneficiaries were the mutual funds" (emphasis mine).

In other words the growth of the mutual-fund industry and the stock market boom was fueled by all the 401(k) (and IRA and 403(*b*) money entering the market.

And the sky seems to be the limit. Note:

"(T)here are now more than 65 million 401(k) accounts, which allow participants to invest in stocks and bonds, often with matching funds from

> *employers—all at a lower cost (to the employer) than the pension plans that 401(k)s replaced. The accounts helped spark a financial-industry boom,* ***funneling billions from under retirement savers' mattresses into mutual funds and the stock market"*** (emphasis mine).
>
> —*Time*, October 16, 2008

Just imagine the glee on Wall Street as they realized what they could do with the 401(k) legislation. Consider the following from the *60 Minute* episode:

> *When employers began to turn 401(k)s into retirement plans the financial community was not shy about promoting them as such. The prospect of trillions of dollars in the hands of unsophisticated investors opened the door for all sorts of potential abuses... The fact is that the typical 401(k) investor is a financial novice...* ***And we give them a list of 20 or 30 mutual funds with really, really powerful names which make it sound like, that is where I want to have my money*** *[the quality of the mutual funds are] mediocre...* ***With half the funds on the list really dogs and should not be on the list to start with*** (emphasis mine).

"There clearly has been a raid on these funds by the people of Wall Street and it has cost the savers and the future retirees a lot of money." US Rep. George Miller, former Chairman of the House Committee on education and Labor.

Before going on to the next chapter, I want to point out two aspects from what has been stated so far.

The first is that by shifting retirement funds from employer pension plans to individual 401(k) plans, we have created a situation **where no one is held accountable for the systematic or catastrophic loss to this country's retirement plans.** In the past, corporations had to make the monthly pension payments to their retired employees. As a result they had to be prudent about where they invested the retirement money. This is one reason why cash value life insurance was a cornerstone of company pension plans. The 401(k) not only spelled the decline of the corporate pension plan but also gave rise to the placement of those retirement plans into the casino called Wall Street.

Today, it is estimated that only 7% of employees have private pension plans, down from 62% in 1980 (when the 401(k) began). While there are some $3.5 trillion in 401(k) plans, almost all are on Wall Street and in mutual funds.

The "parallel tracks leading to the sky" has no safety net when it comes crashing to the ground.

The second point is alluded to in the 60 Minutes program wherein it is stated, "we give them a list of 20 or 30 mutual funds." Wall Street very shrewdly made enrolling in the 401(k) plan extremely easy. The Fidelitys, Vanguards and T Rowe Prices of the financial industry sold corporate America on the idea that not only would they be able to stop funding their pension plans and put much less into employee matching 401(k) plans, but also that it would be easy for the employees to sign up and have their money professionally managed (or mismanaged). All employees had to do was sign a few forms and their retirement plan would be automatically created, managed and grown.

In fact, according to the Pension Protection Act of 2006, employers are allowed to automatically enroll their employees in 401(k) plans thus requiring the employees to actively opt out if they do not want to participate. In addition the employers can arrange the plans so they have no financial liability for investment losses as a result of the automatic enrollments.

This "hands off" approach to personal retirement planning meant that not only was Wall Street able to grow the mutual fund industry while having the investor bear all the risk, but also that the exorbitant fees that they charge would not be scrutinized by the average employee investor.

This combination of market risk, high and often undisclosed or on scrutinized fees, plus the great possibility of future tax increases (which we will discuss in the next chapter), is why the 401(k) is broken as we will see.

But investors have short-term memories and Wall Street loves that.

In March 2010, as the recession was fading and the market was going up, financial advisors across the country found themselves getting phone calls and emails from clients wanting to get back into the market. They did not want to miss the great rally that was taking place.

Many of these same clients had called in the middle of the night two years prior, as Lehman and Merrill Lynch were crashing and the market was plunging and the bottom was dropping out of the economy. Back then, they'd wanted out of the market, and fast. *Sell everything. I never want to be in the market again. I can't handle this anymore.* Now, with the DOW Jones twice what it had been at its nadir and still on the uptick, they urgently wanted back in.

Such is life for those who choose to save for retirement by investing in mutual funds, market funds or stocks and bonds. They buy and hold, for better or worse, unable to move their investment out to cash if the market tanks—and the market *will* tank.

Since 1968 there's been a crash roughly every six to eight years with an average loss of 33 percent. Somebody saving for retirement for thirty years can look forward to weathering three to five such storms. If the crash happens at the right time and you're already out of the market—you've retired, you've moved to cash, you've moved to annuities or CDs—you're good. But if you're like Fred, you're caught in the teeth of it, and you keep on working.

Some people can deal with this uncertainty and risk. Others can't. They cry when they open their statements. Or they don't open them at all; they bring me their statements still sealed up inside envelopes dating back six months and say: "I can't open these. I know it's bad, let's do something about it."

Is the stock market worth all this? A lot of people would tell you it is. The idea that long-term investors are better off taking chances is practically written in stone in the financial-services industry.

But the numbers tell a different story. They tell Joe's story or Fred's story, one whose moral is that making money begins and ends with not losing it, that moderate returns uncompromised by any losses outperform a volatile market over time.

Believe the numbers, not the 401(k) apologists. If you do, you'll avoid emotional distress as well as financial.

How do I know?

I know because not one of my clients called or emailed me in the middle of the night during the 2008 crash. Not one of them ever has. They feel as peaceful tonight, in bed, as they will 30 years from now, in retirement, because they have their nest egg or retirement money in TAX FREE cash value life insurance or fixed-indexed annuities, which come with no market loss guarantees. Consequently, they avoid the major drains that can severely compromise their ability to realize gains. These drains are: market corrections, taxes and early withdrawal penalties, fees and, for the ultra conservative investor, inflation.

I HAVE THE RESULTS OF YOUR STRESS TEST, AND TO BE ON THE SAFE SIDE, I WANT YOU TO STOP LOOKING AT YOUR 401K

Chapter 2

Why The 401(k) Is Broken

There are three main reasons why the 401(k) is broken.

1. **Stock market risk**. Specifically the risk of a major market downturn or catastrophic loss. This is especially devastating in the years immediately preceding or during your retirement while you are no longer contributing to and also withdrawing money from your 401(k) plan thereby not having the time to wait for the market to (hopefully) correct itself and build your account balance back up again.

The stock market went **down 56%** from October 9, 2007 to March 9, 2009. If you were planning to retire in 2009 and you had just lost 50% of your nest egg you would have been in a world of hurt! **<u>Do you want that risk?</u>**

For this reason *TIME Magazine* said *"The ugly truth is that the 401(k) is a lousy idea, a flop, a rotten repository for our retirement reserves."* TIME 10/19/09 in the cover story "Why it's Time to Retire the 401(k)."

The reason that Time Magazine gave for concluding that the 401(k) "is a lousy idea," is stated in the article as follows, *"the biggest factor in whether the 401(k) works as designed has to do with when you retire. If the market rises that year, you're fine. If you retired last year (i.e. in 2008 when the market went down 38%) you're toast.*

When is it a good time to retire?

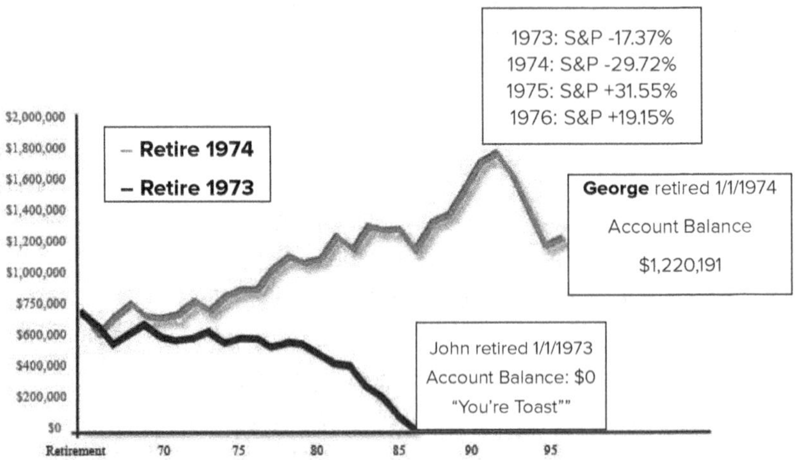

George and John: Both retired at age 65. Both lived until age 95. Both had $750,000 at retirement. Both withdrew 5% ($37,500) per year of the original $750,000.

The above chart tells us the story of two friends (from Liverpool England) John and George. Both had $750,000 in their retirement accounts when they retired at age 65. Both had expected to withdraw $37,500 per year from their retirement accounts.

John retired on January 1, 1973 while George retired on January 1, 1974. During John's first two years of retirement the market, represented here by the S&P 500 Index, went down 17.37% and

29.72%. As you can see John never fully recovered from this almost 50% loss in his retirement accounts even though the market went up over 50% the next two years (31.55% in 1975 and 19.15% in 1976).

George on the other hand retired on January 1, 1974. So even though he suffered one large loss the large gain in the following two years enabled him to continue withdrawing the money he had intended.

In reality, John would have stopped withdrawing money at the same rate of $37,500 per year once he saw that his account was dwindling. The question this graph requires us to ask is the same question we have asked already; do you want to risk this scenario during your retirement?

Wall Street and your stockbroker will tell you that yes, the markets go down, but they will go up again. This may be true and you may make your money back even after a catastrophic loss (in Chapter 3 we will discuss how hard it is to make up money once you have lost it in the market) however this hypothetical story of George and John and the very real story of Joe (our Wal-Mart employee) from the introduction illustrates how **not everyone is able to wait for the market to correct and rebuild their retirement accounts**.

For example, take the case of John Greene of Edgerton, Wisconsin. Greene was the subject of the N.Y. Times article on September 11, 2012, titled "Should the 401(k) be Reformed or Replaced."

Regarding Greene the article stated that:

> ...when the financial markets plunged four years ago, his 401(k) dropped...."We lost more than 70 percent,"

> he complained, even though a highly recommended investment firm was managing his 401(k). "They're very risky."
>
> For Greene, 77, the money he withdrew each year provided him and his wife some breathing room—and comforts—on top of the $29,000 they receive annually in Social Security and pension payments.
>
> But though it has rebounded a little, his nest egg has declined so much that he withdraws far less than he used to. The result: "We can't do trips like Scotland anymore," he said.

Isn't there something wrong with a retirement plan that allows this to happen?

2) **Higher Income Tax Rates in the Future.**

I have already quoted the former Comptroller General of the United States stating that he believes we will have to double income tax rates over time. The truth is that while I could probably fill the rest of this chapter if not this entire book with statements by those who believe that taxes will be much higher in the future, no one knows what the future tax rates will be. However there is ample reason to believe that given the current debt crisis we face in this country, income taxes in the distant future will be much higher than they are today.

This is especially so if we consider that **we are currently at historically low income tax** rates as the following graph indicates.

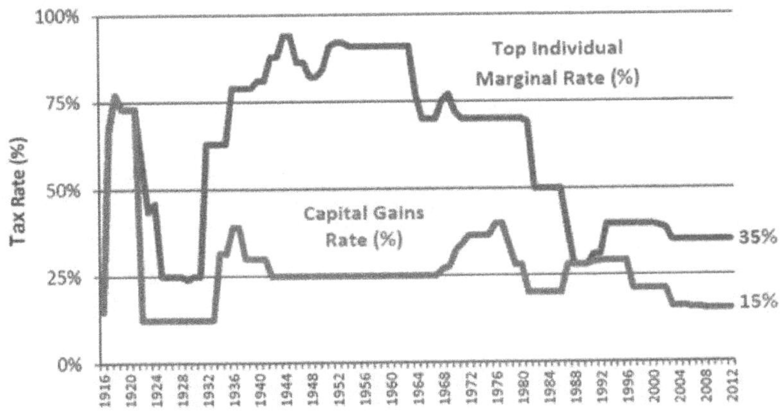

Recently the top tax rate has gone from 35% to 39.6% and capital gains rates have gone from 15% to 20%. In addition the Medicare surtax of 3.8% can bring the capital gains rates up to 23.8%. Dividend tax rates for some have gone from 15% to a whopping 39.6% and if you add the 3.8% surtax on to that it means that some investors will be paying 43.4% on their dividend income. In 2013 there is also the beginning of the phase-out of personal and dependent exemptions and itemized deductions.

As you are aware, when you withdraw your 401(k) or IRA or 403(b) money in the future when you retire, the amount of withdrawals each year are taxed as ordinary income. The logic has always been that when you retire you will be in a lower income tax bracket. But what if that is not true? What if you will be in a higher income tax bracket when you retire because the brackets have gone up?

Add to the above the likelihood that when you retire you will have less deductions such as the mortgage deduction and dependent deductions. All of this means that your 401(k) plan might be deferring into higher tax rates. Remember, tax deferral is really just tax postponement.

3) **Exorbitant (and Often Undisclosed or Hidden) Fees**.

On June 19, 2008 Bloomberg News did a story entitled "The Truth Behind Hidden Fees in 401(k) Plans." The program earned Bloomberg its first Emmy Award. In a summary of the program Bloomberg stated:

> *What many [retirees] will learn, according to the AARP, is the average balance for Boomers nearing retirement is $60,000, due in part to hidden fees that can, over a lifetime of savings,* ***skim off more than half*** *of a 401(k) investor's potential returns.* (emphasis mine).

On the program itself Mike Schneider (the host) states:

> *Many of the fees, all of them legal, are buried in the fine print of obscure documents or are so confusing, they might as well be written in a foreign language... by the U.S. Department of Labors count there are at least 17 different fees that can be charged to your plan. Right now you would be lucky to find even one of them identified on your account statement.*

The program then goes on to profile a Gerry Schneider of Washington State, who lost $44,000 in his 401(k) plan ($422,000 down to $389,000) from January1, 2008 to March 31, 2008, This loss, "like the other 50 million 401(k) investors in America" was the amount Gerry was aware of but he was not aware of the fees he was paying. The company running his 401(k) plan (John Hancock Financial Services), stated that in 2007 they charged annual fees of 1/10th of 1% of the assets in his portfolio or $404. In actuality it was discovered that he had paid $14,558 or about **3.6% of the assets in his plan.**

Bloomberg also interviewed Edward Siedle, former attorney in the SEC's Division of Investment Management and a nationally recognized authority on pensions, investment management and securities matters. He said that in many plans he audited investors were paying **3%-5%.**

In the October 7, 2010, edition of Forbes magazine, Siedle called the 401(k**) "America's Biggest Investment Fraud"** and wrote: *"In my opinion, which I have shared with the SEC, it ought to be illegal to call a 401(k) plan a "retirement plan" and those parties who promoted them as retirement plans should be held accountable."*

What is more amazing is that not even employers know about these fees. Consider the following from MSN Money August 17, 2012, in an article entitled "Is Your 401(k) Ripping You Off?"

> *The companies that administer 401ks have been so good about* ***obscuring costs*** *that 71% of workers polled for AARP believed that they didn't pay any fees for their plans... What's worse, a lot of employers don't know how much their workers are paying. For example: Investment management fees make up the bulk of total 401(k) expenses, according to a study issued by the Government Accountability Office. Yet half of*

> *the employers the GAO surveyed either didn't know if they or their workers paid investment management fees, or they thought that such fees were waived.*

401(k) fees have become such a scandal that on July 1, 2012 the Department of Labor began requiring 401(k) investment companies to provide clearer 401(k) fee breakdowns to employers who would then relay that information to the employee. The problem is, however, that the disclosures are not personalized for each employee. And it is unlikely that employers will take the time or will have the ability to explain them to the employees.

Note the following from an ABC News article on November 8, 2012 by Anthony Kippins:

> *But, as is often the case with new regulations, the federal rules aren't having the intended effect—at least not yet. Instead, the large companies that provide these plans are testing the regulatory waters by disclosing fees in account statements in* ***less-than-transparent ways****, making it extremely difficult for employees to figure them out.*

Or this from Market Watch:

> *New Department of Labor regulations went into effect this year requiring plan providers to disclose the amount in fees that both companies and their employees pay for their 401k plans. The intention was to shed light on notoriously murky 401k fees. But critics have been disappointed with the first round.*

Some statements "disclosed" a wide range of fees, as in "your expenses range from 0.25% to 2%," leaving companies wondering where exactly their fees stood. This is no accident, critics charge. "They didn't try to make it plain English and fail, they complied with the letter of the law and made it as gibberishy as possible." Greg Carpenter, the CEO of Employee Fiduciary, an independent administrator of 401k plans.

So the 401(k) is broken. It is subject to catastrophic market risk, future tax increases and exorbitant and/or hidden fees. Is there a retirement vehicle that solves these problems? Yes there is. However, we first need to take one more swipe at Wall Street, specifically in the way they analyze and report average returns.

REMEMBER, HAMLET, IT'S NOT WHAT YOU HAVE IN LIFE THAT'S IMPORTANT...
CHRIS BROWNE 5-16
IT'S WHAT YOU HAVE LEFT AFTER THE GOVERNMENT TAKES ITS SHARE THAT'S IMPORTANT!

Chapter 3

Math Does Not Equal Money[1]

If you had $100,000 in an investment and in one year it went down 20%, you would have $80,000. If in year two you made 24% you would have $99,200. From a mathematical point of view the 20% loss and 24% gain means that you made 4% over the two-year period or you averaged a gain of 2% per year. **In actuality you lost $800.**

Let's take the above scenario the other way. If you have $100,000 in an investment and in the first year the investment makes 100%, you would now have $200,000. If in the second year the investment loses 50% (of the $200,000) you would have $100,000 (the same number you started with). Again, from a mathematical point of view you made 100% and lost 50% so that is a 50% gain or 25% per year. **In actuality you broke even**.

1 I first heard this phrase from Merle Gilley of Triquest Equity Management in Virginia.

Wall Street and your broker will tell you that in the first scenario above you averaged a gain of 2% per year and in the second you averaged a gain of 25% per year. In reality, you lost $800 in the first case and broke even in the second.

Before explaining the reason for this and the implications let me give you one other example. Look back at the chart at the end of the Introduction. If you add up all of the positive numbers that the S&P 500 returned (19.51% in 1999, 26.38% in 2003 etc.) you have gains of 121.48% over the 14 years. If you then add up the losses (-10.14% in 2000, -13.04% in 2001 etc.) you have 85.05% in losses. If you subtract 85.05% from 121.48% you would have a total return of 36.43% or an average gain of 2.6% over the 14 years (36.43% /14 = 2.6%).

However, if you had actually made 2.60% each year (so after the first year your $100,000 becomes $102,600 and after the second year it becomes $105,208 etc.) then at the end of 14 years you would have had $143,240. But as the chart indicates, in actuality you would have had only $112,102 or an average return of 0.86%.

The reason for this disparity is the difference between what is called the arithmetic mean and the geometric mean. The 2.60% is the arithmetic mean or "average" return and the 0.86% is the geometric mean or "actual" return. **The actual return and the average return will NEVER be the same if you have to factor a negative number.**

To put that another way, whenever you have to factor in a negative number you cannot simply add up the positive numbers and then subtract the negative numbers and divide by the amount of units you have. You need to make up the negative first and that brings down the total yield.

Wall Street is constantly advertising rates of return, but you should always be aware of what they are showing. Often, they are not giving you the real picture.

Chapter 4

If I Had a Crystal Ball

Let's pretend that you are sitting at your desk on Sunday, January 3, 1999. Because the S&P 500 Index had gone up by at least 20% in each of the previous four years, you were thinking of putting $100,000 of your retirement nest egg money into an S&P 500 Index Fund. The fund would track the S&P 500 in both the gains and losses.

All of a sudden I call you on the phone and tell you that I know of an A rated company that will manage your money in a similar way. They will take your $100,000 and track the S&P 500 Index. However there are three differences between their management account and the one at your broker.

The first difference is that anytime the S&P 500 returns a loss, you would **not get that loss** but rather you would get a 0% return. The second difference is **that in return for this no loss guarantee your gain will be capped at 14%.** In other words, if the index goes up 30% you will only get 14% and if it goes up 11% you will get 11% (i.e.,"up to" the cap). This is what the company calls a "0% floor and a 14% cap." This also means that in any year you get a gain credited to your account, that gain is locked in and your account is reset at that number and you can only go up from there. This is called the "lock and reset" provision. The third difference we will deal with later.

Initially you are not certain if this is a good idea or not because in the years 1995 through 1998 the S&P 500 Index went up 34.11%, 20.26%, 31.01%, and 26.69% (from January 1 through December 31). You would never have needed the no-loss guarantee, and you would have given up everything above 14%. However, I tell you that I have a crystal ball, at least in regards to the annual S&P 500 returns through 2012 (i.e. I have the chart from the Introduction). Because you are excited to use your new email technology (remember this is early 1999) you ask me to email you over the chart.

Upon looking at the chart and noticing the double-digit losses to come in 2000, 2001, 2002 and 2008 you realize that it would probably be a good idea to take advantage of the "zero floor guarantee."

You would, of course have been correct. The following page has the same chart reproduced with the additional columns showing the 0% floor/14% cap strategy. Before looking over there and seeing the effect of the new strategy take a guess at what the ending account balance would be. Remember the December 31, 2012 balance in the S&P 500 Index Fund is going to be $112,702

Performance of $100,000 in an S&P 500 Index Fund from January 1, 1999 to December 31, 2012 vs. an account with a 0% floor and a 14% cap. (Not including fees or taxes or possible dividends reinvested)

YEAR	Actual S&P 500 Performance Jan 1-Dec 31	S&P 500 Account Value	0% Floor/ 14% Cap Account	Account Value
1999	19.51%	$119,500	14.00%	$114,000
2000	-10.14%	$107,383	0.00%	$114,000
2001	-13.04%	$93,380	0.00%	$114,000
2002	-23.37%	$71,557	0.00%	$114,000
2003	26.38%	$90,434	14.00%	$129,960
2004	8.99%	$98,564	8.99%	$141,643
2005	3.00%	$101,521	3.00%	$145,892
2006	13.62%	$115,348	13.62%	$165,762
2007	3.53%	$119,420	3.53%	$171,613
2008	-38.50%	$73,443	0.00%	$171,613
2009	23.45%	$90,665	14.00%	$195,639
2010	12.80%	$102,270	12.80%	$220,681
2011	00.00%	$102,270	0.00%	$220,681
2012	10.20%	$112,702	10.20%	$243,190
14 year Total	0.86%	$112,702	6.72%	$243,190

You see that by avoiding the losses, even while capping the gains, you **end up with $243,190 as opposed to $112,702 in the regular S&P 500 Index Fund account.** Now I am not saying that in every 14-year period you will more than double your money in this type of an account. **The above simply illustrates the need to avoid loss especially in your retirement nest egg account**.

You are pretty sold on this idea and while contemplating it you asked me what the third difference between this company and a typical S&P 500 Indexed account is? I tell you that this A-rated company has a special deal with the IRS that all of the gain earned in the fund is **tax-free.** Not only that but you do not even report the gain on your 1040 tax return. Even better, unlike a traditional IRA or 401(k) where the distributions are taxed as ordinary income, **with this account the distributions are taken out tax-free.**

Before you have a chance to react to that bit of news, I tell you two other pieces of information from my crystal ball. One is that inflation will continue to be 2.7% over the next decade.[2] The other is that soon 10 year CD rates will be under 2% and money market rates will be under .05% (and the Federal Reserve would come out and say that they intend to keep rates low for many years).

"Wow" you say, no risk of market loss, an average gain that clearly beats inflation,[3] a high cap of 14%, and all tax-free. "What's the catch?" You ask.

I tell you that while I don't think there is a catch, this account is for those who understand that good things come to those who wait.

---

2 According to an online calculator at www.usinflationcalculator.com, the same goods I purchased for $100,000 in 1999 would cost me $137,811 in 2012. This 37.8% rate of inflation over the 14 years would be an annual inflation rate of 2.7%

3 If you take every 15, 20, 25 and 30 year period since 1930 and apply a 0% floor and 14% cap, your worst average return would be **7.83%.**

Chapter 5

Suze Orman and Dave Ramsey are Right, Except When They Aren't

Lyle Alzado was one of the most dominant football defensive linemen of his era. He played for the Denver Broncos, the Cleveland Browns and most famously for the Oakland Raiders. He was the 1977 Defensive Player of the year, made the NFL Pro Bowl in 1977 and 1978, was the 1982 Comeback Player of the Year and won the Super Bowl with the Raiders in 1983. He was big, he was fierce and he was immensely strong.

He also died at the age of 43 from brain cancer, which he said was due to his steroid use.

Growing up a Bears fan in Chicago in the late 1970s there was not much to cheer about except Walter Payton's record-breaking runs. So I followed the Oakland Raiders and John Madden, Ken

Stabler and, of course, the ferocious Alzado. What a shock it was to see him on the cover of the July 8, 1991 edition of Sports Illustrated looking so frail. His open admission of using steroids and his well-documented illness ushered in the current age of anti-doping laws in professional sports.

However, as bad as anabolic steroids are, not all steroids are bad or unhealthy. For example corticosteroids combat inflammation from disease infection and other causes. Fluticasone is used to control and prevent symptoms caused by asthma. It works by reducing swelling or inflammation of the airways in the lungs to make breathing easier.

I mentioned this perspective on steroid use because the type of account that we saw in the last chapter which offers a guarantee against market loss (0% floor), a double-digit earnings cap (14%) and entirely tax-free growth and distributions is a very specific type of life insurance policy called which is structured or "funded" in a unique way.

Notice that I did not say that this is simply cash value life insurance. Rather it is **a specific type of life insurance structured in a specific way**.

When most people hear about life insurance as a cash value accumulation vehicle they hear Suze Orman and Dave Ramsey and others telling them that it's a bad idea. We will deal with this opinion, which has some merit, in a moment. For now, however, it is important to understand that not all steroids are bad, and in the hands of the right person, for example a doctor, they are very beneficial. So too is life insurance. The proper type of insurance in the hands of an agent who **knows how to properly structure**

a policy for cash accumulation, can be very beneficial as a tax-free retirement vehicle.

Suze Orman, Dave Ramsey and your stockbroker (who probably does not want you taking money out from under his or her management) do not like life insurance as a way to build cash value because they think it is too expensive. Before discussing or analyzing their position let me briefly point out two basic aspects of life insurance.

First of all as you probably know there are two types of life insurance. Term life insurance and permanent life insurance. Under the permanent life insurance category there are two general categories: whole life and universal life (there is also Variable Life but we are discussing life insurance with cash value guarantees). This is important to understand. I know several insurance producers who will tell you that the two types of life insurance are term life and whole life. But this is incorrect. Whole life is a subcategory of permanent life insurance and understanding the difference between whole life and universal life is crucial to our discussion.

The second thing I want you to be aware of is something called Net Amount at Risk (NAR). If a person has a permanent insurance policy with a $1 million death benefit and a cash value of, say $300,000, and that person dies, his heirs do NOT get the $1 million of death benefit plus the $300,000 of cash value. Rather, the beneficiaries will get $1 million consisting of the $300,000 that the person had in their cash value plus $700,000 that the insurance company will pay to them. This $700,000 is called the Net Amount at Risk to the insurance company because this is the amount of money that the insurance company has to come up with to pay the claim.

We will discuss the expenses associated with a permanent life insurance policy the next chapter. For now just remember that the greater the Net Amount at Risk is to the insurance company, the more expensive the policy. Of course there are 2 ways to reduce the Net Amount at Risk. One is to lower the death benefit (so the company doesn't have to pay out as much in a death claim) and the other is to increase the cash value (so the company doesn't have to pay as much of their money in a death claim).

With term life insurance you are only buying the death benefit for a specific term. There is no cash buildup in the policy and the term will end at some point in the future. This type of insurance is much cheaper than permanent life insurance.

With whole life insurance you are also purchasing death benefit. However, some of your premium goes into a cash account that will earn a dividend when the company declares a dividend. This purchase of the death benefit is a major cost or "drain" on the policy and is thus not a very efficient way of building up cash in a policy. This is Dave Ramsey's and Suze Orman's complaint against whole life insurance as a way to build up cash value. Why pay for the life insurance when you don't need to? It would be a lot more efficient to "buy term and invest the rest." That is, buy a cheap term life insurance policy to cover you in case of a sudden death, and put the rest of the money into an investment for your retirement. (Discussing the investment vehicles they suggest, which are often subject to market risk, is not the subject of this book.).

As a life insurance producer I will tell you something that may surprise you. Regarding cash value growth **I agree with them**. Whole life insurance is a very inefficient way of building cash. First of all the cost of insurance is quite high because you are usually buying a lot of life insurance. (Here's a little secret, usually the more life insurance death benefit you buy, the greater the commission for the agent). Second, the dividends credited to your cash account are controlled by/or decided to be given to you by the insurance company. Third, the fees, costs and other expenses associated with a whole life policy are typically not revealed to the policyholder. Because the fees are not revealed, the policyholder and his or her agent, have less control over them.

This is not to say that whole life insurance is always a bad idea. Sometimes it is the best thing for a person. What the Suze Ormans of the world do not realize is that there may be very valid reasons for buying whole life policies, depending on the situation of a particular individual. For example, if a person feels they do not have the discipline to "invest the rest" that strategy will not work too well. On the same side of that coin, if a person feels that they will quickly withdraw money from an investment account, but they are unlikely to withdraw money and lapse their whole life insurance policy, then whole life insurance might be a good option for them. Another example would be a person who is extremely worried about future tax rates being much higher and wants to take advantage of the tax-free nature of life insurance. Each person's situation is different.

In "Safe Money Millionaire," Kitchen and Kap profile a number of famous people such as JCPenney, Walt Disney and Ray Kroc who used the money in their cash value life insurance policies to help start their businesses. However, I assume that these policies were not sold to them primarily for the cash value. Rather, they kept on funding their whole life policies and when they needed it most the cash value in those policies was there for them.

However **the basic premise of whole life insurance being an inefficient way of building cash <u>is correct</u>**. I liken this to heating your house with space heaters. You CAN heat your house with space heaters and there may be times when it is necessary to do so. An example of this is if the boiler blows out. However it will be very expensive to heat your house this way.

However, what if there was a tax-free life insurance policy where you could customize, or dial down **or suppress the life insurance portion to the minimum possible**?[4] And what if you could further **reduce the fees** in the policy by funding it in such a manner that lowers the policy costs to the bare minimum by reducing the Net Amount at Risk? And what if you could further look at the fees and costs and expenses of the policy to make sure that they were as low as possible? And what if you could have the cash value portion of the policy earn money not based on declared dividends from the insurance company but rather with the robust strategy we saw before with a 0% floor and 14% cap[5] (all tax free)? In other words what if you could make the cash value portion of permanent life insurance into a very efficient heater?

To use the other analogy, what if you could use life insurance to create a tax-free and market risk free retirement plan on very powerful and beneficial steroids?

---

4 As we will see, the IRS has certain rules about the minimum amount of life insurance you need to buy in a policy in order to keep it a "life insurance" policy and thus tax-free versus an "investment" which can be taxable. The goal, of course, is to keep the policy tax-free.

5 Different insurance companies have different caps, currently ranging from 10% to 14%.

Welcome to the solution to the broken 401(k).

Welcome to Indexed Universal Life or IUL.

IUL is a much more flexible or customizable insurance policy where we can suppress the death benefit portion and use other methods to lower the fees of the policy while putting the rest of the money into the cash value account. By working with an advisor who is proficient in IUL, you can fund the policy in the most efficient manner while also keeping the policy tax-free according to IRS guidelines. (A full discussion of the Internal Revenue Code sections and pieces of legislation that are at work in this area is beyond the scope of this book[6]).

6 The relevant sections of the Internal Revenue Code are IRC sections 101, 72e and 7702. The pieces of legislation are TEFRA (1982), DEFRA (1984) and TAMRA (1988).

Chapter 6

Yes, There Are Fees, but They Are Lower Than Your 401(k) Fees and Much Lower Than the 'Fee' of a Market Correction

There are fees associated with an IUL contract. In fact, depending how you structure the contract, fees can be quite significant especially in the first several years of the policy. To be specific there are three sets of fees.

1) **Premium Loads**: This is the amount taken out of your premium every time you make a payment into the policy.
2) **Cost of Insurance**: This is the amount taken out to buy the life insurance death benefit. This death benefit not only provides protection for the insured but also keeps the policy tax-free according to IRS rules.
3) **Other Fees and Expenses**: This is the money that goes to the company to pay commissions, salaries and to invest for the policyholder's, including the bonds and conservative option strategies that the insurance company uses.

Several things need to be kept in mind when looking at these fees:

1) **IUL is first and foremost life insurance**. This means that this fee that we call cost of insurance is not just a fee that is given to a broker but it goes towards purchasing valuable life insurance.
2) One of the reasons why the insurance company is able to give up to a 14% cap is because they are using a good amount of your cost of insurance money to **purchase conservative option strategies.** So, some of the fees you pay are really going to help you earn more money in your cash value account.
3) As stated before, the fact that this is life insurance **keeps the account tax-free** (if structured according to IRS guidelines). **How much would you pay to guarantee a tax-free growth and distribution account?**
4) Unlike your 401(k) plan, these fees **are entirely transparent** and are shown on the expense report before the policy is signed.[7] Not only do you know the fees that you will be paying but you can work with an advisor who knows how to minimize these fees. (See the next chapter for discussion of whether these fees can change or not).
5) Finally, as will be shown shortly, over time the **fees in an IUL policy are much smaller** than the fees in a 401(k) plan. (Which as we pointed out in Chapter 2 is already a scandal).

7 I am critical of an IUL life insurance company (or agent) that does not produce the expense report as part of the illustration but rather has it as a separate report that the producer must print out. I believe that just like the client has to sign the illustration they should have to sign the expense report (which should clearly add up the columns).

AYE, AYE, SIR! WE CHECKED OUT THE 401(K) FEES AND THERE'S NOTHING TO BE CONCERNED ABOUT.
CORPORATE RETIREMENT PLAN
401(K) FEES
HIDDEN FEES

401(k) fees vs. IUL fees

Male 35 Years Old

$17,500 into a 401(k) for 30 years until age 65

vs.

$13,125[8] into an IUL for 30 years until age 65

IUL: NOT Optimized for Cash: Initial Death Benefit $1,122,057

Assume Both Accounts Earn 7% Annually

Age	Annual 401(k) Fees at 1.5%	Total 401(k) Fees	401(k) Balance (TAXED on Withdrawal)	IUL Fees	Total IUL Fees	IUL Balance (TAX FREE)
35	$263	$263	$18,444	$3,736	$3,736	$10,261
40	$1,803	$6,036	$126,709	$4,612	$25,328	$56,818
45	$3,807	$20,854	$267,503	$1,894	$46,098	$132,195
50	$6,413	$47,434	$450,603	$2,322	$56,717	$264,170
55	$9,802	$89,310	$688,718	$2,650	$69,129	$452,163
60	$14,209	$151,078	$998,379	$3,027	$83,412	$723,096
65	$19,678	$238,454	$1,382,639	$3,491	$98,803	$1,115,384
70	$35,308	$397,820	$2,480,826	$5,115	$121,401	$1,595,812
75	$45,916	$605,071	$3,226,237	$5,098	$148,282	$2,286,429
80	$59,713	$874,594	$4,195,620	$9,733	$186,228	$3,282,653
85	$77,655	$1,225,100	$5,456,277	$19,460	$261,245	$4,693,043
90	$100,980	$1,680,923	$7,095,720	$41,820	$419,631	$6,660,987
95	$131,331	$2,273,706	$9,227,764	$10,311	$565,741	$9,463,328
99	$162,050	$2,873,811	$11,386,140	$517	$595,662	$12,710,942
Total		**$2,873,811**	**$11,386,140**		**$595,662**	**$12,710,942**

Illustration A (not optimized for cash value; see Note 1 below)

8 Payments made into a life insurance policy are NOT tax deductible. The $13,125 represents the after-tax equivalent of $17,500 in a 25% bracket. Instead of contributing $17,500 into a 401(k) plan and getting a tax deduction of $4,375, you would hold out the $4,375 to pay the taxes and put the difference of $13,125 into the IUL.

401(k) Fees vs. IUL Fees

Male 35 Years Old

$17,500 into a 401(k) for 30 years until age 65

vs.

$13,125[9] into an IUL for 30 years until age 65

IUL: Optimized for cash; initial death benefit $391,064

Assume both accounts earn 7% annually

Age	Annual 401(k) Fees at 1.5%	Total 401(k) Fees	401(k) Balance (TAXED on Withdrawal)	IUL Fees	Total IUL Fees	IUL Balance (TAX FREE)
35	$263	$263	$18,444	$1,914	$1,914	$12,084
40	$1,803	$6,036	$126,709	$2,400	$13,011	$68,371
45	$3,807	$20,854	$267,503	$942	$24,171	$161,923
50	$6,413	$47,434	$450,603	$1,338	$29,950	$311,506
55	$9,802	$89,310	$688,718	$1,898	$38,097	$526,208
60	$14,209	$151,078	$998,379	$3,168	$50,785	$833,669
65	$19,678	$238,454	$1,382,639	$5,338	$72,767	$1,270,610
70	$35,308	$397,820	$2,480,826	$5,807	$98,855	$1,815,597
75	$45,916	$605,071	$3,226,237	$5,788	$129,374	$2,601,407
80	$59,713	$874,594	$4,195,620	$11,062	$172,485	$3,734,946
85	$77,655	$1,225,100	$5,456,277	$22,129	$257,774	$5,339,741
90	$100,980	$1,680,923	$7,095,720	$47,570	$437,920	$7,578,942
95	$131,331	$2,273,706	$9,227,764	$11,719	$604,100	$10,767,552
99	$162,050	$2,873,811	$11,386,140	$575	$638,091	$14,462,807
Total		**$2,873,811**	**$11,386,140**		**$638,091**	**$14,462,807**

Illustration B (Optimized for Cash Value: See note 1 below)

9 Payments made into a life insurance policy are NOT tax deductible. The $13,125 represents the after-tax equivalent of $17,500 in a 25% bracket. Instead of contributing $17,500 into a 401(k) plan and getting a tax deduction of $4,375, you would hold out the $4,375 to pay the taxes and put the difference of $13,125 into the IUL.

I would like to highlight a number of points about Illustration A and Illustration B above. Before I do, however, it must be pointed out that the above illustrations are entirely hypothetical. You will not actually earn 7% each year either in your 401(k) or your IUL account. Some years your 401(k) will earn 20% and in some years, as we saw before, it may lose 20%. Similarly, some years the IUL will make 14% (i.e. the "cap") and some years it will yield a 0% return (the "floor").

Also, the above illustrations do not include possible dividend reinvestment of the 401(k) growth, nor do they include possible employee matching of the 401(k) (Many employers no longer match 401(k) contributions). Finally, I have made these illustrations showing no income coming out of either the 401(k) or the IUL. This is significant because as we will see later on in Chapter 8, one of the best things about an IUL plan is the way you access your tax-free income. This additional benefit is not illustrated above.

1) Illustration A vs. Illustration B.

Illustration A is "not optimized for cash value." This means that we have NOT tried to lower the death benefit to the minimum amount allowed by IRS law (to keep the policy tax-free). Rather we have elected a higher initial and level death benefit of $1,122,057. **This often makes sense** if a person wants the additional death benefit (most people, especially with children, are underinsured) while also getting a very good rate of return on a tax-free and market risk free basis. Because more money is going into the death benefit portion, the Cost Of Insurance (COI) is greater and so the total initial fees are greater (first-year fees of $3,736 vs. $1,914 in the optimized plan of Illustration B).

Illustration B, on the other hand, IS optimized for cash value accumulation.[10] Here we lowered the death benefit to $391,064 because that was the **bare minimum amount** of life insurance we needed to buy in order to keep the policy **tax-free according to IRS guidelines**. This causes less Cost Of Insurance (COI) charges and thus less drag on the policy (the Net Amount at Risk to the insurance company is lower). The difference is significant and provides over $150,000 more money by age 65 (i.e. $1,270,610 in the cash optimized plan versus $1,115,384 in the non-optimized plan).

2) IUL beats the 401(k) hands-down (and with no market risk). Tax on the seed vs. tax on the harvest!

By age 65, the 401(k) has $1,382,639. However removing this money (either during retirement or if you pass away and your heirs take out the money) **will be a taxable event**. A 25% tax rate will reduce that figure to $1,036,980. Both the optimized and non-optimized IUL plans provide significantly more on an entirely tax-free and market risk-free basis. This is called paying tax on

10 In truth, **we CAN optimize this policy even further** by putting in the same amount of money in larger amounts over a shorter period of time. That would reduce the Net Amount at Risk faster and lower the Cost Of Insurance (COI). However for the sake of this 401(k) vs. IUL comparison, we are funding this over 30 years.

the seed ($4,375) versus paying tax on the harvest ($345,659).[11] Also, with the IUL plan there is **a significant tax-free death benefit the minute you make your first premium payment into your policy.**

3) What are the 401(k) fees?

In Chapter 2 we met Gerry Schneider of Washington State. Gerry was the person that Bloomberg News profiled. He thought that he was paying 1/10 of 1% for his 401(k) fees (that's what he had been told) but in actuality he was paying 3.6% per year. I have seen 401(k) fees estimated at anywhere from 1.5% per year to 4.5% per year, so I believe that using **1.5% in the illustration above is conservative**.

However we can never really be sure what the 401(k) fees are. Consider a report in US News on May 25, 2012 quoting from the Government Accountability Office (GAO) report which stated ... "*because sponsors of plans of all sizes may not be aware of certain fees that participants are paying, such as transaction costs and wrap fees, it is difficult to get a clear understanding of the total fees that participants are actually paying.*"

Obviously if we assume a greater fee structure for the 401(k), the IUL plan will do even better in comparison.

11 Imagine a farmer who purchases $1,000 worth of seed at the beginning of the season with the hope of turning that into $100,000 of wheat by the end of the season. If given the option, he would rather pay a tax of $250 (i.e. 25% of $1,000) on the seed, rather than a tax of $25,000 on the harvest.

Keep in mind that unlike 401(k) plan fees (and unlike many other fees that you are subject to on Wall Street) **every dime of your IUL fees is stated up front** in the expense report that you can (and should) review before you sign a policy. (In Chapter 7 we will deal with whether these fees can change.)

This transparency in IUL (in the insurance industry this is often referred to as "unbundled") is also a difference between IUL and whole life insurance. With whole life you do not see the fees beforehand (and as stated earlier what you get credited to the cash value of your policy is not determined by a market index,[12] but rather by whatever the company decides to give you).

4) 401(k) fees $2,800,000 vs. IUL fees $500,000. You Decide.

The main point of these illustrations is to show that the 401(k) fees are significantly higher than the IUL fees. It is true that in the initial years of the policy, when the insurance company has to buy a death benefit for you, the fees ARE higher. However, by age 50 (i.e. 15 years into the policy) the cumulative 401(k) fees (at a conservative 1.5% per year) are significantly higher than the IUL fees ($47,434 vs. $29,950).

And if you did hold both accounts until age 99 without taking income the total fees you would have paid in your 401(k) account

12 I want to make it clear, that with an IUL policy, your money never goes into the market. The company just uses the index to determine how much they are going to credit your cash value.

would be more than four times what it would be in an IUL ($2,873,811 vs. $638,091).

5) The IUL balance is not the surrender value.

Notice the last column titled "IUL Balance (TAX FREE)". That $12,084 is the value of your account that is earning the 14% if the market goes up that high or 0% if the market goes down (or somewhere between 0% and 14% if that is what the market yields).

However that is NOT a "surrender value." That is, if you actually wanted to take out your entire account and cancel your policy you **would** be subject to a significant surrender charge in the first several years of the policy. The insurance company needs to purchase life insurance on you and also needs to go out and purchase a secure bond (often a long-term US government bond), which they will have to break if they need to give you all the money back. So while you can certainly take out a significant amount of your balance at any time even in the first few years, you cannot cancel your entire policy without being subject to large surrender charges.

It is vital to understand that an IUL policy is not meant to be cashed in or even significantly withdrawn from in the first few years of the policy. A general rule is that before beginning withdrawals you want to have **eight to ten years** for the policy to make up some of the upfront fees and cost of insurance associated with the policy. You also want to have enough years for the policy to earn some of the caps, i.e. the 14% (depending on the carrier). This does not mean that you cannot take out an occasional amount even in the first few years, but the more you take out in the early years the more strain (or lag) it puts on the policy.

Note that there are some IUL carriers that have riders to their contracts, which eliminate the surrender charges, and even **guarantee a return of your entire premium at any time**. Obviously there are costs for these riders, but if early liquidity is important to you they are available.

Of course a typical 401(k) plan also has significant early withdrawal penalties in the form of the **10% pre-59 1/2 withdrawal penalty**. Also, as we have seen, a typical 401(k) plan subjects you to the greatest potential "fee" of all which is catastrophic market loss.

IRA's also can have large fees!

Even if you have a traditional IRA and not a 401(k), you are probably paying exorbitant fees in the form of mutual fund costs and advisory fees.

> *In over 25 years of business, our firm has never had an initial meeting with an investor who completely understood the total costs of the mutual funds they owned. Ty Bernickle of Bernickle & Associates, Eau Clair, Wisconsin*[13]

13 Forbes.com "The Real Cost Of Owning a Mutual Fund." April 4, 2011

TYPICAL MUTUAL FUND COSTS

1) **Annual Expense Ratio** (AER): i.e., the fund's fee (operating expenses & management & Advertising Fees-also 12b-1fees).. **1.23%**[14]
2) **Annual Assets Under Management** (a.m. Fee: i.e., the advisor's fee.. **0.90%**[15]
3) **Annual Trading Expenses or Transaction Costs** i.e., the fee taken out of the account when the security is bought or sold.. **1.44%**[16]

Total Costs and Fees.. **3.57%**

Notice that these are NOT 401(k) fees. They can apply to a traditional IRA as well as any account.

---

14 Based on all Mutual Funds and ETF Tracked by Morningstar as of 12/31/11

15 Based on Rydex Advisor Research Study of 561 advisory firms (2009)

16 Based on 1,706 S.A.I. (Statement of Additional Information) reports in a study by Virginia Tech, University and Boston College (2007). Note: this S.A.I. report is usually not given to the client unless asked for specifically!

Chapter 7

Can the Caps and Fees Change?

Can the caps and fees on an IUL policy change? In other words, can you purchase an IUL policy today with a 14% cap and a 0% floor and fees and costs that you reviewed in the expense report, and in 10 years have the policy change to a cap rate of say, 8% and a floor below 0%, and greater fees and expenses?

The answer is, like almost everything else in life, yes there can be SOME changes. The caps can go down or they can go up. The same is true with the fees and costs. This is why it is important to work with an advisor who works with insurance companies that have excellent "in force cap renewal histories." **There ARE insurance companies that have either not lowered caps at all on any in force policies since before the "great recession" of 2008- 2009 or have lowered them only 1/2 a percent (from 14.5% to 14%).** On the other hand, I know of another carrier that has lowered in force cap rates more than 2% in that time.

The same thing goes for fees and costs of insurance. Because people are living longer, often the cost of insurance can go down (the longer people live the less risk to the insurance company and the less costly the policy becomes), however, contractually speaking the company CAN raise costs of insurance, fees and expenses just like they CAN lower the cap on a policy.

A good insurance carrier that understands IUL pricing sets the initial cap and fees on a policy so that they will not have to change. Not every insurance carrier does this well and it is important to work with one that does. Furthermore, when caps are lowered they are typically lowered by half a point or a point so it is unlikely that your 14% cap today will be an 8% cap ten years from now.

Having said all of that it is important to point out **two things that cannot change** in an IUL policy. The first is that the floor of 0% cannot be lowered. In other words, no matter what happens **the cash value of your policy cannot be subject to stock market losses.** And second, your policy will always be **tax-free** (if structured properly).

Of course, everything else can change. The stock market can go down close to 40% like it did in 2008, or go down by double digits three years in a row like it did in 2000, 2001 and 2002. And it can do this in the years immediately preceding your retirement when you may not have the luxury of waiting for the market to come back for you. And of course, like we saw before, taxes can go up in the future.

IUL protects you from all of these potentially catastrophic and expensive changes.

When discussing IUL the important question is not "is it expensive?" or "can the values change?" Rather, the question you need to ask is, "is it expensive compared to my other retirement planning options?" Or "can it change more than my other retirement strategies?"

Let me ask you this:

How expensive is a 30% to 40% market decline?

How expensive are taxes? And how expensive will they be in the future when you withdraw your 401(k) or IRA income?

How expensive are the fees you are paying in your 401(k), 403(b), IRA or other mutual fund account? That is if you can find all the hidden fees in some of these accounts.

How expensive is that 10% pre-59 1/2 withdrawal penalty if you need to get to your retirement money early?

How expensive are the required minimum distributions (RMD's) that you need to begin taking from your qualified plans (and pay taxes on) beginning at age 70 1/2 whether you need the money or not?

Now ask yourself:

How much value is there in an account when you cannot lose money to market decline (while potentially earning double-digit returns)?

How much "value" is there in an account where the growth and distributions are all tax-free?

How much value is there an account with lower fees (when structured properly) which are all transparent?

How much value is there in an account with no 10% early withdrawal penalty and no required minimum distributions?

How much value is there in a tax-free death benefit that is in existence the minute you sign your policy?

And finally,

How much value is there in being able to use your policy to borrow money at say, 6% and potentially earn 14% on the money you borrowed?

Oh, I did not tell you yet about one of the greatest benefits of an IUL policy. Read on....

Chapter 8

The Amazing Way YOU GET Your Money

When it comes time to take money out of your IUL policy, there are 3 basic ways to do so. 1) Withdrawal; 2) Fixed Loan; or 3) Index Loan

In order to illustrate these three ways let us use the following example.

Let's say you put $10,000 per year into an IUL policy for five years. This $50,000 is called your basis in the policy. Assume further that your 50,000 has grown to $100,000 and that the life-insurance death benefit from the beginning was and still is $500,000.

In this example you want to buy a new car and you need $30,000 to do so. You could pull the money out of your other savings that are earning interest, or you could take a car loan from a finance company and pay interest to them. Or you could use your policy's cash value.

1) **Withdrawal**: You can call up the insurance company and ask for a withdrawal of $30,000. There is no charge for doing this and there is no penalty for doing this. The company will send you $30,000 and then your cash value will be worth $70,000 and your death benefit will be worth $470,000 (i.e. each reduced by the $30,000 withdrawal you took from the policy). You cannot repay this money back into the policy and there is no tax on this money because it is a return of your money (i.e. your basis).[17]

Most of the time withdrawal is not the most efficient way of taking money out of your policy.

2) **Fixed Loan**: (Sometimes called a wash loan, a zero cost loan or a preferred loan). Instead of withdrawing money from your policy, you can decide to take a loan and be charged an interest rate. This is where many advisers and insurance agents are unclear. When the company loans you money they do NOT loan you your own money and charge you for that. That would not be fair. Rather they take $30,000 from their general account and loan you that money. They use $30,000 of your $100,000 of cash value as collateral for the loan. This means that the entire $100,000 of cash value **REMAINS IN YOUR POLICY**.

If at this point you passed away (without having repaid the $30,000 which you do not have to do) your heirs would get the $500,000 in death benefit **(tax-free)** less the $30,000 loan

[17] Note that if you would withdraw $60,000 i.e. $10,000 more than your basis, you would be taxed on the $10,000 gain. For this reason you would switch to a loan after you removed your basis.

balance that you have to pay back to the insurance company for a total benefit of $470,000. Also, you are able to repay this $30,000 back into your policy if you want to.

If you do not repay the loan, the company will charge you an annual interest rate on the $30,000. This rate will be fixed at 3% (for example). The good news is that with many insurance companies you can choose to have that $30,000 be credited in the cash value at the same 3% rate. So while they are charging you 3% for the money, they are also crediting you 3%. This is why it is called a "wash loan."[18]

The other $70,000 in your cash value will still be earning the 14% cap/0% floor depending on market performance.

3) Index Loan: (Sometimes called a variable loan.) An entire industry has been built around this concept. If you ever hear advertisements on the radio for "Bank on Yourself" or "Infinite Banking," they are referring to this idea.

Like we saw with the fixed loan, the $30,000 remains in your policy and is subject to an interest rate. The **index loan** interest rate will be higher than the **fixed rate**, say 6% for example (some companies cap this rate for the life of the contract, so you can never be charged more than this).

The loan "charging" rate (the 6%) is higher with an index loan because you agree to let the $30,000 participate in the 0%

---

18 Some companies do not allow "wash loans" for the first few years of a policy. If this is the case then the fixed loan rate they charge you would be 4% (for example) while the credited rate you earn is 3% for a total loan charge of 1%.

floor/14% cap strategy. This means that **while you will be charged 6% on the $30,000 you can make 14% on that money** (if the market goes up to or beyond 14%). This potential for an 8% "positive loan arbitrage," is what makes an index loan so dynamic. See the graphic on the next page.

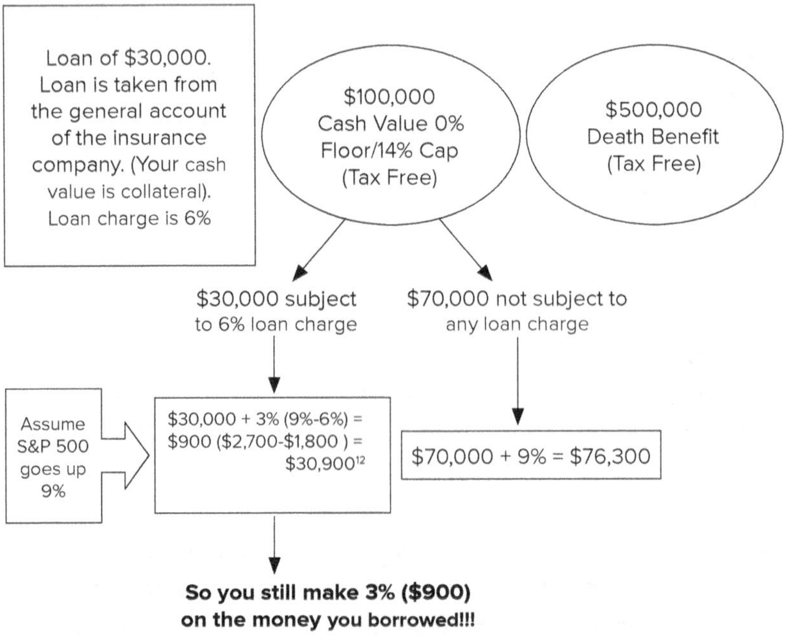

Note: If the S&P goes down, the floor of 0% applies and your account would be charged 6% of $30,000 or $1,800 with no gain to offset this amount.[19]

[19] The idea here is that the insurance company will charge your account $1,800 (6% of $30,000) per year and in the year when the S&P 500 goes up 9% they will credit your account that much (up to the cap of 14%). You would end up with a $900 gain even though you borrowed that money from the company.

But it gets even better than just being able to make money on the money that you borrow. This is because you can repay the loan back to the insurance company and back into the 0% floor/14% cap strategy. This means that instead of borrowing the money and paying the interest to a finance company, you can **pay the interest to yourself**. This is what is known as "Be Your Own Bank." or B.Y.O.B.

> *By borrowing from your policy to pay cash for cars and other big-ticket items and making loan payments back to the policy, you get back the money you pay for those items and recapture interest you now pay to finance institutions.* Bank on Yourself, by Pamela Yellin.

To recap, IUL offers the following:

- Tax-Free Growth and Tax-Free Distributions
- Absolutely No Market Risk
- Potential Double Digit Growth[20]
- Ability to borrow on your policy and still earn interest on the money you borrow
- No pre-59 1/2 withdrawal penalty and no age 70 1/2 required minimum distributions
- Immediate tax-free death benefit (it IS life insurance after all)

[20] Since 1980 (33 years) this strategy (0% floor & 14% cap) would have returned double-digit yields in 18 of those years; between 1% and 9.99% in 8 of those years; and the 0% floor in 7 of those years. The average return would have been 8.34% (from Jan 1-Dec 31).

Chapter 9

Why Doesn't Everyone Do This?

At this point you should be asking what many of my clients ask. "Why doesn't everyone have one of these IUL's?" After all, it's tax-free, market risk free, potential double digit growth, has an average gain of over 7%,[21] has lower fees than the average 401(k), gives you the ability to take out index loans in order to earn money on the money that you borrowed, plus there is a life insurance death benefit. Also, in most states, the cash value of a life insurance policy is creditor protect.[22]

---

21 If you go back with the S&P 500 Index to 1930 and apply a 0% floor and a conservative cap of 12% (many of the top IUL carriers have caps between 13%-14%), the lowest average yield you would have returned in any 15, 20, 25 or 30 year, would have been 6.98%

22 There are many other benefits to an IUL contract depending on the carrier. For example, several insurance companies allow you to use the death benefit while alive for long-term care insurance. Basically, the insurance company will advance you your death benefit to pay for healthcare costs. With some companies this is a free rider and with others there is a charge. This is a great way to take care of your long-term care insurance needs.

So why is it that more people do not have IUL policies? Why is it that you probably have never heard of this concept?

There are several factors to explain this.

The first is that an IUL is <u>not</u> an unknown or new item or a hidden strategy. They have been around since the mid 1990's. At the end of 2007, there were 34 companies that issued Index Universal Life policies. At the end of 2012 there were 48 such companies. 2011 sales of IUL were 39.93% greater than 2010's sales.[23] Since 2012 IUL sales have been more than $1 Billion every year. According to LIMRA (Life Insurance and Marketing Research Association) in 2015, IUL "represents 20% of all individual life premium." As you can see, we are not speaking about an unknown concept.

Also, note the following from the Wall Street Journal on June 5, 2010, titled, Juicing Your Life Insurance, by Leslie Scism, the Journal's News Editor in Personal Finance and Insurance.

> *This year's hottest life-insurance product is well suited to an era of sudden "flash crashes" and overall uncertainty: It appeals to people eager to capture stock-market gains while avoiding undue risk. The product—"indexed universal life....*

But it is true that IUL sales are dwarfed by the estimated $3 trillion or more in 401(k) plans almost all of which are at risk on Wall Street in mutual funds. We have already seen the reason for this.

---

[23] Data courtesy of annuityspecs.com's indexed sales and market report.

The 401(k) industry is huge. Every day people see advertisements in publications from Forbes Magazine to Time Magazine to their local newspaper telling them to put their 401(k) money in one of the major investing houses such as Vanguard, Fidelity or T. Rowe Price etc. We have already spent a good deal of time talking about the fees that are generated from these accounts. Wall Street is not giving up these fees to the insurance industry anytime soon.

Moreover, the fact that the 401(k) plan is a "de facto" retirement plan means that an employee has his or her retirement money going into Wall Street via automatic enrollment. This is the only way to explain the continued growth of 401(k) plans even after the mega losses they sustained just a few years ago.

Add to all of this the Suzy Ormans and Dave Ramseys of the world telling people not to put money into cash value life insurance (again, you cannot lump all cash value life insurance in the same basket) and you understand why IUL sales have not taken over as the primary retirement vehicle in this country (like they should be).

The other reason why you may never have heard of Index Universal Life is because most life insurance agents do not understand "high cash value/low death benefit" life insurance. Most insurance agents sell whole life policies with the maximum death benefit and view the cash value portion as a future benefit that will be there for the client if necessary.

I have spoken to many experienced life-insurance agents who view Universal Life as another form of Whole Life but with a greater number of crediting methods for the insured and higher "caps." In other words, instead of making money only when the company declares a dividend, with Index Universal Life the money earns interest based on the performance of an external market index with a double digit cap (like 14%). While this is true of Indexed Universal Life, it is **by far not the main feature. Suppressing the death benefit, structuring the policy to lower the fees, and using the right carrier is far more important**. Most agents are not proficient in these techniques.

Also, in most cases insurance agents make more commission the more death benefit they sell. So a life insurance concept like IUL that **lowers the death benefit** is not as appealing to many agents.

As you can see, while IUL is not rare or unique, the combination of the 401(k) being the de facto retirement plan with automatic enrollment, plus the "financial gurus" of the word telling people not to put money into cash value life insurance plus the fact that many insurance agents are not familiar with IUL, creates a situation where IUL is not as popular as it should be.

Silent Spring

In 1962 Rachel Carson wrote the classic book Silent Spring. The book exposed the hazards of the pesticide DDT and changed the way we look at pesticides and chemical treatment of our environment.

Imagine that 50 years ago, DDT was liberally sprayed throughout the environment, cigarette smoking was considered safe, margarine (hydrogenated oils) was considered healthier than butter and asbestos tile and pipe wrapping (which is now known to cause mesothelioma), was used throughout industry and school systems in this country.

DDT, cigarettes, hydrogenated oils and asbestos are just some of the many ideas and trends that have been proven to be a total failure. **I believe, as do many others, that the 401(k) belongs in this category**. And while the 401(k) debacle does not rise to the same level of bad as lung cancer, I know that Joe, who we met in the Introduction, does not like having to go back to work being on his feet all day at Wal-Mart.

It is my hope that this book and several of the other publications that have come out promoting Index Universal Life (see Appendix 2 for a list of other sources) will help both the consumer and the insurance agent further the process of moving nest egg or retirement money which should be kept safe, off of Wall Street and into Index Universal Life (IUL) insurance.

Chapter 10

Beware of Biased Advice; and Your Responsibility

My father, of blessed memory, to whom this book is dedicated, was an eminent psychotherapist as well as a world-renowned theologian. He taught me many things. One of them was that it is very difficult to get unbiased advice. Whether financial or personal, emotional or spiritual, most people have an agenda or at least a bias that will influence their opinion and their advice.

Your stockbroker or money manager is no different.

Let me tell you about a client of mine, we will call him Don.

Don came to me to do his estate plan (will, trust and powers of attorney). He was 54 years old, divorced with 2 children and held a steady job.

After we finished his estate plan I told him about Indexed Universal Life and he thought the concept was outstanding. I gave him some background material and various web sources to investigate the product and we scheduled another meeting. At that meeting, we went over the specific amount that he would put into his policy and over how many years and that he would take out his money when he was close to 70 years old.

He was very interested and then he said the words that I knew would kill the sale. He said, "I want to see what my financial advisor has to say about this."

You should understand that the term "financial advisor" could mean two different things. Some financial advisors manage money and sell stocks and securities and make a management fee or commission when they do so. Other financial advisors sell life insurance and annuities and make a commission on those products.

As an insurance salesperson I am of the latter type. Don's financial advisor was of the stockbroker/money manager type.

So, while Don's actual words were "I want to see what my financial advisor has to say about this," what I knew he was really saying was "let me show this to my financial advisor/money manager/stockbroker for what I believe is an unbiased objective opinion, so that he can tell me how bad it is to put money into life insurance so that he can keep or "conserve" the money under his management."

I called Don about a week later to find out if he wanted to proceed with the IUL and he did not return my call. I sent him an email a few days later, which he responded to as follows: "Thanks for the information. I realize that I am making 17% on my funds now so I will have to pass." I responded to him that if he is making greater than the cap on the IUL policy (17% versus 14%) and he is comfortable with the level of risk he is taking, than he should of course stay where he is.

In truth, I do not believe that Don was really making 17% on a consistent basis. Had he been I think he would have told me earlier. I think what actually happened was that his money manager convinced him that IUL was a bad idea and so he told me something I could not really argue with.

Of course, Don's financial advisor was biased and I don't think Don realized that. If he had realized it, I think he might have been more objective and would have made his own decision.

Your Responsibility

We began discussing the three-legged stool that had been the cornerstone of this country's retirement planning. Way back when, a "hands off" approach to your retirement plan was acceptable. Your company pension was going to be there for you as was Social Security. The stock market was not so volatile[24] so your personal savings was also safe.

24 On November 1, 1978 President Jimmy Carter said "the day before yesterday, the stock market went up more than it ever had in history, **over 35 points.** That's an indication of confidence in our government."

Things are different now. Company pension plans are not as common, Social Security may not be there for you or certainly not in the way you may have anticipated,[25] and if your personal savings is on Wall Street or in mutual funds you know the risks that can be associated with those investments.

Because of what has happened to the 401(k) industry we have entered an environment of "hands on" retirement planning. This means that you need to take an objective and thorough look at your retirement plan despite what the financial gurus and stockbrokers tell you.

Annual Review

I hope you will seriously consider looking into starting an IUL plan for your retirement. If you do, you still have the responsibility of reviewing your plan each year. The insurance agent that sells you the plan should conduct an annual review with you to make sure that the caps and fees are remaining steady so that you do not have to lower the insurance death benefit (thereby lowering the fees you pay into the policy).

Also, in unlikely event that the index goes down in the first several years of your policy (meaning you make 0% for several years in a row) while the fees are being withdrawn, you may need to adjust your policy's death benefit or wait longer to begin withdrawals.

[25] Several sources have Social Security running out of money within 10 to 15 years.

Legal Reserve

Before ending this work I would like to deal with one other objection I sometimes hear when selling life insurance in general, and Index Universal Life, in particular. That is, is life insurance safe? What about AIG?

First, it is important to understand that AIG is not only an insurance company. American International Group owns many financial subsidiary groups such as a banking division, a brokerage division, a money management division and a life insurance division (and some others). Their life insurance division was never at risk of not paying out claims.

Of great importance is the need to understand that all A-rated companies that issue IUL policies are what are known as **"legal reserve" companies**. That is, they are life insurance companies which operate under state insurance laws which specify the amount of reserves the company must maintain **at all times** to pay claims. Banks or brokerages do not have this requirement, which has the effect of letting you know that there will always be money to pay your claim.

Along these lines, refer to the discussion we had in Chapter 6 regarding insurance policy fees. Realize that some of the fees you are paying into the policy are going to the reserve fund of the insurance company so that they can maintain the reserve requirements.

Keeping your money safe and tax-free in an Index Universal Life policy makes good sense.

Chapter 11

Funding College

One year of tuition, fees and room and board at a private college today averages more than $42,000, according to the nonprofit College Board.

That's more than $169,000 for a four-year degree.

State schools are less expensive but at all not cheap, averaging almost $19,000 a year for an in-state student.

And if your child opts for a public college in another state, well—brace yourself to shell out almost $33,000 a year.

College expenses have been rising twice as fast as inflation, according to the Consumer Price Index. Student debt in the U.S. has skyrocketed as the college-bound scramble for loans to pay their way. But parents remain the single biggest source of money for college, footing more than a third of the bill, according to 2014 research by student loan lender Sallie Mae.

An IUL could be of help.

Certainly it beats a 529, which has four problems:

1) The amount of money in your 529 plan goes on your FAFSA. It counts against you insofar as it's considered an asset;
2) There are tax consequences if you don't use it for an approved college. So if you decide to go to a trade school or an overseas college or a much less expensive and ever popular online college, or if he or she elect not to go to college at all, that money is taxed and penalized;
3) There are fees. The 529 plan is in mutual funds. It's in the market;
4) There are market losses, just as with your 401(k) plan.

What if 30 years ago you started putting money in a 529 plan (assuming there was such a thing then), and your kid was getting ready to go to college and the market tanked. Instead of having $70,000 for college, now he/she might have only $35,000. What would happen there? It's one thing for our friend Fred the bank manager to say, "Okay, I'll continue working. It's my business." It's another thing for him to have to tell his kid: "I've got bad news. You've got to go to a community college."

Or what if he or she decides to go to a trade school or an overseas program that's not an accredited college. You've got to tell them, "I put this money away for you, but it's locked up because you've got to use it for only these colleges." Why play around with Johnny's dreams?

The other possible catastrophe with a 529 plan is something happens to you—a car crash, cancer, whatever; you have what you've contributed and that's it. Had you done an IUL, however, the half-million dollar death benefit would more than pay for college.

A better way to pay for college than a 529 is to do what we call a Section 7702 college-savings plan starting when the child is newborn or very young. That's tax-free, cash-value life insurance (IUL). Let's say you put in $500 a month for the child's college education over 15 years starting when the child is born. That amounts to $90,000 put in, which is NOT included on the FAFSA and so doesn't count against them for financial aid. This level of funding also comes with over $500,000 of tax-free death benefit if the parent passes away. Based on historical performance this IUL account could provide $35,000 per year for 4 years of tuition money (over $140,000 of benefit) while still allowing the child to get financial aid. But unlike a 529 plan, if the kid decides not to go college, the parents have the money, and it's tax-free; it's a cash-value life insurance policy. So that's very good.

Not everybody goes to college. If I need my money from my 529 plan and it's restricted to being used for college, that's a problem. An IUL avoids this problem because it's your money and unrestricted.

And if the parent is the main breadwinner and also the life on the policy and that parent dies early then the life insurance death benefit can be used to pay for the child's college tuition.

Furthermore, when the child gets married, the parent can simply say to the child "I have a wedding present for you. You don't have to go out and buy life insurance. I've got a half-million dollar policy, and I'll change the beneficiary from your mother to you or your spouse."

Timing is crucial, though. Say you're a junior or senior in high school and you meet with a financial planner trying to tell you to take your money out of your investments and sort of hide it in life insurance so it's off the FAFSA. You have to be very careful about that. It can backfire. That's not what this is. This is starting when the child's younger and *saving* for his or her college.

Chapter 12

Fixed Indexed Annuities

As great as Indexed Universal Life (IUL) insurance is for building tax-free money with no stock market risk, it does have a few limitations.

The first is that you cannot put qualified (IRA/401(k)) money into an IUL policy (or any life insurance policy for that matter). If you currently have money in a qualified account you would have to take it out as a distribution and pay tax on that money and then you could put that into an IUL policy. While this may be desirable for some people (especially if you need death benefit protection) the extra tax burden may not be desirable for others (see appendix 1 for an advanced strategy as to how to deal with this).

The second drawback to and IUL policy is that the cash value account performs best if it is left alone to allow for several years of growth. As a general rule at least 5 and preferably 10 years of interest credits is advised. The reason for this is because the costs of insurance (COI) in the first few years of the policy limits the cash value growth. See Chapter 6. (Although some insurance companies do have riders where you can get all your money back any time). So if you intend to begin taking out your money in the first few years, an IUL may not be your best option.

A Fixed Indexed Annuity (FIA) can help with both of these scenarios. This is because qualified money can be rolled over from an IRA or 401(k), which is at risk in the market, into an FIA with no tax consequence. Not only that, but many FIAs have "lifetime income riders" which guarantee you lifetime income no matter how long you live. Guaranteed lifetime income is important because of something called longevity risk, that is the real fear that you might run out of money if you live a long time. These riders, often for an extra fee in the policy, can allow you to begin taking lifetime income immediately or perhaps after waiting one year. Obviously, the longer you leave your money in the annuity the more annual lifetime income you will have, but unlike an IUL policy it may often be advisable to take the lifetime income beginning in the first few years of the policy.

FIA's have some interesting similarities with IULs. Both are issued by insurance companies (often the same insurance company that issues an IUL also issues annuities). Also, the same indexing strategy where there's the floor of 0% and a cap applies to the FIA. However, there is no life insurance death benefit with FIA and the FIA caps are significantly lower than in an IUL policy. Also, the growth in the annuity contract is tax-deferred (of course if the money is already in a qualified account it is already tax-deferred) but unlike the cash value life insurance policy, when you withdraw money you pay taxes similar to an IRA or 401(k).

The good news is that recently several independent research firms have said and studies have been done proving that Fixed Indexed Annuity rates of return are competitive or even outperform stock market returns and this is all on a no market loss basis (the floor is 0%).

1) An article produced by FRC (Financial Research Corporation) which is an independent research firm stated that "**income annuities generate more income per dollar of capital invested than any other income generating asset class, are non-correlated with equity and bond markets [i.e., do not have market risk] and perfectly hedge longevity risk-a powerful combination of features to address a significant set of challenges.**

2) In an article entitled "Real – World Index Annuity Returns." The authors claim that this "paper offers the first empirical explanation of fixed indexed annuity returns based on actual contracts that were sold and actual interest that was credited." They conclude that **"the returns of real – world index annuities analyzed in this paper outperformed the S&P 500 index over 67% of the time and outperformed a 50/50 mix of one year Treasury bills and the S&P 500 79% of the time."**

3) An article in *Time* magazine entitled "Lifetime Income Stream Key to Retirement Happiness." stated that "Annuities sold through big insurance companies like New York Life, Allianz and John Hancock have soared in popularity as retirees have come to understand that guarantee lifetime income makes them more financially competent – and happier, too."

4) A Wall Street Journal article entitled "the Case for Income Annuities," discussed a study released by the University of Pennsylvania's Wharton Financial Institution Center and stated that 2 professors concluded:

> An income annuity is the only asset class the two professors found that most effectively addresses the risk of outliving your nest egg, because it generates a permanent stream of income, unlike a typical nest egg of stocks, bonds and cash. Meanwhile, the study notes, investors who place retirement wealth in mutual funds "are subjected to greater risk, typically higher expenses, and returns that are unlikely to keep pace with annuity returns, when investment risk is taken into account."

Please keep in mind that all fixed indexed annuities have a **no loss guarantee** and therefore really should be compared with CDs and money market accounts, and not to the stock market. However, it is also good to know that they compare favorably or even outperform a much riskier market fund.

Yes, annuities have surrender charges and therefore should be considered longer-term contracts. But let me ask you, if you put $100,000 in the market and it goes down 20% and you need the remaining $80,000, what would you say the market's surrender charge is? There has never been an annuity with a 20% surrender charge. The surrender charges decline as the annuity is held longer and the surrender charges only apply to the amount taken out beyond the 10% penalty free withdrawals. Also, with an annuity contract you are aware of all of the surrender charges and any fees upfront. This is not the case with your typical mutual fund.

TWO ANNUITY STORIES

Sally the Widow

Sally's seen death more than most. She's a nurse.

Recognizing the value of life insurance, she and her husband bought some of their own. When Sally's husband died several years ago, she collected $700,000 in life insurance.

Sally (not her real name) was in her early 60s then. She's now 69 and shouldn't have to worry about money. But recently she started feeling anxious, so she sought help.

Sally is a family friend. She called me one day.

"You do financial planning, right?" she said. "I put $320,000 in the market with a big named firm and a long time financial advisor and it's down to three-hundred and five thousand now, in two months." She was upset and worried.

Now, from a money manager's point of view, a loss of less than 5 percent is not a huge deal. Her financial advisor had even told her not to worry; she had 95 percent of her money left to work with. But this was a widow. To her, the loss meant something, and I knew that, because I knew her and her situation.

I said: "Well we have funds, and we're much more protective. But you may have losing quarters."

And she said, "No, I don't want to lose *anything*."

My late father was a psychologist, so I always understand the emotions of investing and I understood her thinking. In truth, Sally had nothing to worry about either way. She's never going to touch that money. She doesn't need it. She has a pension and social security and her house is paid for and she does not live high. The money will just go to her kids. But I couldn't tell her that. I couldn't say: "Look, Sally, this is play money for you. Let your guy have it. Let it go down until it comes back up. Don't worry about it."

Warren Buffett famously said the only way to get into the market is to be into anything for ten years—never look at anything before ten. If you're not able to hang through the cycle, if you're ever going to look at your money when it's down, you shouldn't be in the market, especially in a 401(k) or an IRA. You should be in something that doesn't go down.

That's all Sally wanted. She wanted total peace of mind. She wanted to never have to look at her statement and see a loss. Left to the cold calculus of faraway strangers, she wouldn't have gotten it. She might or might not have ended up with more money, but in the meantime she'd have felt financially insecure—and that meantime could have ended up lasting most of the life she has left. Even if she finally realizes marked gains after six or 10 years, what would that have meant to her?

Nothing.

So she opted for something that couldn't lose.

"You do annuities, don't you?" she said.

“Sure,” I said, “I do annuities.”

“I want an annuity,” she said

So we moved the remaining $305,000 into an annuity that not only gave her a bonus when she opened up the account but also has a guarantee that the worst she will do is 0% when the index is down while she can get credited up to 8% or even more when the index is up. This annuity has a 25-year historical back tested record of averaging 6.36%. Of course historical returns are no guarantee of future returns but what is guaranteed is that she will not lose. Remember also that Sally has no liquidity needs. An annuity is perfect for her.

Peter the Engineer

Peter is a 62-year-old engineer. He is really sharp and really detailed oriented. Besides other investments he has $450,000 in his 401(k) with his employer. Peter came to me because he was thinking of taking early retirement in a year or 2 (his company was going to pay him to do this because they can hire someone younger for less money than they are paying him). His goal was to retire in 2 years, sell his home here in Chicago and moved to Myrtle Beach South Carolina and play golf all day.

The cornerstone of his goal was his $450,000 nest egg 401(k) and he was extremely worried about what he saw as a very volatile market and what that might due to his retirement fund. Peter is very healthy and his parents lived well into their 80s so he expects to live a long time. Guaranteed lifetime income is precisely what he was after.

I told him that if he rolled over his 401(k) into a Fixed Indexed Annuity, not only would he get a 10% or $45,000 bonus immediately credited to his account but he could attach the income rider for an annual fee, which will allow him to begin taking $32,000 per year for the rest of life starting at age 66. This will continue no matter how long he lives. When we got to crunching the numbers he realized that he would have to earn close to 6% per year in the market without a loss in order to achieve the same lifetime income results.

Of course the annuity is a long-term contract and as we said before, there is a penalty for withdrawal beyond the annual 10% penalty free withdrawal. But Peter has other money and he never expects needing more than 10% per year from his annuity. So the FIA with the guaranteed lifetime income rider was perfect for him.

I tell you the stories of Sally and Peter because they each have 2 things in common. Firstly, an IUL policy was not for them. Sally never wants to see a reduction in her account value and in the 1st few years of an Indexed Universal Life (IUL) policy the cash value is less than you start with. This is due to the cost of insurance and other fees in the policy as we have mentioned. And Peter wanted to begin taking income in the 1st few years of his policy so a Fixed Indexed Annuity (FIA) with a guaranteed lifetime income rider was a better option. Also, Peter's money was already in a qualified plan (a 401k) so he would have had to to pay tax if he took out his money in order to purchase cash value life insurance.

The 2nd thing that Sally and Peter have in common is that the annuity was a right fit for them. Neither had liquidity concerns and both wanted absolute financial peace of mind and got that in the annuity.

Ken Fisher Hates Annuities and I Hate Brussels Sprouts

Ken Fisher, of Fisher investments, is a 30-year *Forbes* columnist, owner of his money management investment firm, best-selling author and according to Wikipedia is worth $2.7 billion. Obviously the man knows what he is doing.

Many had seen Ken Fisher's full-page advertisements in dozens of publications and online which says that he hates annuities. Now I hate Brussels sprouts, and although my wife, God love her, has gotten me to eat many vegetables, the hated Brussels sprout will never cross my lips as long as I am conscious.

Here is my question. Why does Ken Fisher spend millions and millions of dollars advertising to you that he hates annuities and I don't spend one thin dime to tell you about the vegetables I like or do not like? The answer is because Ken Fisher wants to stop you from putting money into an annuity, or he wants to assist you in taking money out of an annuity, so he can get money under management in his firm Fisher Investments. Of course, every one of his advertisements carries a disclaimer that you can lose money in the market. This you will never see on an annuity because there is no market risk.

Of course it is wrong to lump all annuities in one basket as Ken Fisher does. Variable Annuities, where your money is actually at risk in the market, are very risky financial vehicles. But the bigger point I am making is that Ken Fisher really loves annuities because it gives him a whole asset class that he can bash and criticize to get money for him and his investment advisors.

In my opinion, your nest-egg retirement accounts should be safe in a TAX FREE IUL policy and if that is not for your situation then you should seriously look into a Fixed Indexed Annuity. And of course, please eat your vegetables.

Note: For a video explaining how FIA's and Income Riders work please go to www.incomeridervideo.com

Table I

IUL vs. IRA/401(k)

	IUL	IRA/401(k)
IRS Approved	Yes	Yes
Tax Status	Tax Free	Tax Deferred
Average Annual Rate of Return	7%[1]	Market
No Market Loss Guarantee	Yes	No
Contribution Limits	No	Yes
Pre-59 1/2 Withdrawal Penalty	No	Yes
Required Min. Distributions at 701/2	No	Yes
Immediate Tax-Free Death Benefit	Yes	No
Withdrawals Reported on Tax Return	No	Yes
Loans Allowed	Yes	Not Usually
Loan Repayment	Optional	Required
Transparent Fees	Yes	No
Use of death benefit as long-term care insurance (carrier specific)	Yes	N/A
Used for College Funding[26]	Yes	No
Deductible Contributions	No	Yes
Employer Match	No	Sometimes
Creditor Protected	Often	Yes
Probate Free Transfer to Heirs[16]	Yes	Yes

26 Refer to notes 2 and 13

27 Using IUL as a college funding source is an exceptional way to help pay for college tuition. The key is to start the policy early on so there is time to build up cash in the policy. Note that the cash value of a life insurance policy is not included on the federal student aid form (FAFSA). This means that you can build up a large cash value in your policy and still get loans and grants for college.

Table II

IUL vs. 401(k) with Employer Match

Male 35 Years Old (Income of $100,000 Per Year)

$20,500[28] into a 401(k) for 30 years until age 65

Vs.

$13,125[29] into an IUL for 30 years until age 65

IUL: Optimized for Cash: Initial Death Benefit: $391,064

Assume Both Accounts Earn 7% Annually (Net of all Fees)

Age	401(k) Balance	401(k) Balance Less 25% Tax	IUL Tax Free
60	$1,169,529	$877,147	$833,669
65	$1,619,663	$1,214,747	$1,270,610
70	$2,906,110	$2,179,583	$1,815,597
75	$3,779,307	$2,834,480	$2,601,407
80	$4,914,872	$3,686,154	$3,734,946
85	$6,391,639	$4,793,729	$5,339,741
90	$8,312,129	$6,234,097	$7,578,942
95	$10,809,667	$8,107,250	$10,767,552
99	$13,338,050	$10,003,537	$14,462,807

28 Many employers do not match at all. According to the Bureau of Labor Statistics, the most common formula for those that do match is 50% of every dollar up to 6% of salary. For someone making $100,000 this would amount to a $3,000 matching amount. Adding this to the maximum 401(k) contribution of $17,500 gives us $20,500.

29 Payments made into a life insurance policy are NOT tax deductible. The $13,125 represents the after-tax equivalent of $17,500 in a 25% bracket. See footnotes 8 and 9.

Note: The above illustrates that the IUL policy can outperform a 401(k) **even with** an employer match, all on a market risk free basis. In reality, withdrawing your entire 401(k) balance at one time would put you in an even higher tax bracket. Also, not shown is the effect of income withdrawals from this account. With the IUL you could withdraw $120,000 per your tax-free using index loans until age 100. At that withdrawal level your 401(k) account would **run out money at age 83!**

Appendix A

"Converting" Your Current 401(k) or IRA

After reading all of this you might be thinking that IUL is only a great idea for someone in their 20s, 30s, 40s and early 50s because they can let the policy grow before beginning withdrawals. However that is not the case. The main consideration when analyzing whether or not an IUL plan is a good idea has to do with when you plan to start taking out money. A **62-year-old** that will begin taking out money at age 75 may be as good a candidate for an IUL plan as a **35-year-old** who would like to begin taking out money at age 48[30]. One thing that is certain is that the younger the better.

---

30 Often, people in their 60s or beyond have the mistaken impression that they cannot get life insurance. This is not the case. People can get life insurance well into their 70s. Also, the life used in a policy does not have to be the same as the owner of the policy or the beneficiary. For example, the policy owner (who makes the premium payments and takes out loans from the cash value) can be a grandfather, and the life used (upon whose death the insurance benefit will pay out) can be a child, and the beneficiary of the death benefit can be a grandchild.

Many people have current 401(k) or IRA plans and wonder if they can take the money out of those plans and put it into a tax-free, market risk-free IUL. In other words can you "convert" your 401(k) or IRA into an IUL?

The technical answer to this is no, you may not "convert" your current "qualified" plan because "conversion" is a term meaning making an automatic election and changing the status of an account. For example you may be familiar with a Roth IRA conversion. To convert your traditional IRA into a Roth IRA (or traditional 401K into a Roth 401(k) if your employer allows this) all you need to do is call up your IRA custodian (your broker) and tell him or her that you would like to convert your current "qualified" plan into a Roth.

Once the broker notes the account this way, you are the proud owner of a Roth IRA and it is your responsibility to report the converted amount as income on the following year's tax return.

IRA Rescue, and IRA Rescue using IRS Section 72(t)

Fortunately, there are two strategies that allow you to withdraw your money from your current tax deferred IRA/401(k) plan and put it into a tax-free IUL. If you choose you can even do this with no out-of-pocket cost. Which strategy you use will depend on if you are over 59 1/2 or under 59 1/2.

Note that in order to keep the policy tax free according to IRS guidelines you must do this over a number of years.[31]

If you are over 59 1/2, and thus are not subject to a 10% early withdrawal penalty, the steps to an IRA rescue are as follows. For this example assume that you have $200,000 in an IRA or 401(k)[32] and you would like to "rescue" all of it. You and your advisor determine that it is best to do this over five years (i.e. $40,000 per year).

1) Turn $40,000 into cash in your IRA and withdraw it to your personal account. This withdrawal is a taxable event and at a 25% tax bracket it will cost you $8,000 to be paid when you file next year's tax return.
2) Put this $40,000 into an IUL policy. Your death benefit will probably be 1.5 to 4 times the $200,000 that you are going to put in. In other words, you should have an immediate **tax-free insurance death benefit of somewhere between $300,000-$800,000.**
3) When you file next year's tax return, take a loan from your policy in the amount of $8,000 to pay the taxes. As we discussed earlier, this loan will be charged an annual interest rate but does not need to be repaid. If it is not repaid the insurance company will pay the loan back to themselves out of the death benefit they pay to your heirs

31 Basically, if you put too much money into an insurance policy too quickly, the IRS considers the policy an "investment" and no longer an insurance policy and it is then subject to taxes. The goal is to stay under this limit so the policy does not become a Modified Endowment Contract (MEC). You must work with an advisor who understands how to do this.

32 If you are still employed at your company with the 401(k) you need to check and see if your employer allows an "in-service distribution."

after you pass away. Note that if you do not need to take this loan (i.e. you can pay the $8000 tax bill out of your current money), and you can keep the money in your policy, it will grow that much faster.

4) Each year you will repeat steps 1 and 2 until the money is no longer in the IRA and is all in the IUL

It is very important to keep in mind that if you do take policy loans in the first few years of your policy, you must refrain from taking loans for several years thereafter. Again, you must work with an advisor who is familiar with the strategy and how to fund and manage the policy properly.

If you are under 59 1/2 then withdrawing the money from your IRA or 401(k) will result in an additional 10% early withdrawal penalty. This often makes the above strategy less viable (although you can always run the numbers and see if it works given your time horizon for taking out the money). The way to avoid the 10% early withdrawal penalty is to use IRS section 72(t).

IRS section 72(t) allows for pre 59 ½ penalty free withdrawals from qualified plans[33] as long as the withdrawals are taken out as a series of "Substantially Equal Periodic Payments" (SEPP) based on life expectancy. After age 59 1/2, any amount of the IRA can be withdrawn with no penalty (of course the income tax will always have to be paid). Also, once the 72(t) plan begins no modification to the payments and no additional withdrawals are allowed until five years (or 59 ½) is achieved.

---

[33] Again, you will need to check with your employer regarding an "in-service" 401(k) distribution using 72(t).

The steps for this strategy are as follows. Again assume $200,000 in an IRA with someone age 51.

1) Determine the SEPP using an online 72(t) calculator. There are several of these out there but make sure to use one using current rates. Assume for this example the 72(t) amount is $7,000 per year.
2) Each year from age 51 to age 59 1/2 (9 years) you will turn $7,000 into cash in your IRA or 401(k) and withdraw it to your personal account. This withdrawal will not be subject to the 10% early withdrawal penalty. Assume for this example that the small tax this does cause ($1,750 in a 25% bracket) will be paid by personal funds i.e. you will not need to go into your policy and borrow money to pay the tax.
3) Each year you will put the $7,000 into your Index Universal Life policy as the premium. (So after nine years you would have put $63,000 into the IUL)
4) After age 59 1/2 you are no longer subject to the 10% early withdrawal penalty so you can take the amount remaining in your qualified plan (approximately $137,000 not including interest) and feed it into the IUL policy over the next several years. If necessary, you can take policy loans to pay the taxes that the withdrawals will cause.

I cannot stress enough how important it is to work with an advisor who is familiar with these strategies. Often, the "advanced markets" team of a top IUL carrier will need to be brought in on these cases. Issues such as over funding the IUL policy (thus making it a taxable) and reporting requirements to the IRS, must all be taken into consideration.

Appendix B

Other Sources and Information

There are many great books on the subject of Indexed Universal Life, 401(k) problems and fees, the need to avoid stock market risk/safe money investing and using insurance policy loans as a way to build wealth:

The 60 Minute episode on the "401(k) fallout" as well as the Bloomberg News story on "Hidden 401(k) fees" and Time Magazine's editor discussing their cover story "Why it's Time to Retire the 401(k)" can be seen on my site www.401kfallout.com.

Many books have been written on the topic such as:

"Tax Fee Retirement" and "the Retirement Miracle" by Patrick Kelly
"The Better Money Method" by Terry Laxton
"Blind Faith: Our Misplaced Trust in the Stock Market" by Edward Winslow
"The Great Wall Street Retirement Scam" by Rick Beuter
"The Great 401(k) Hoax" by William Wollman
"Bank on Yourself" by Pamela Yellin

"Becoming Your Own Banker" by R. Nelson Nash

In addition, I have several videos on my website regarding IUL in general and the "IRA Rescue" strategy in particular please go to **www.completeerp.com**

For other videos with more detail about IUL and other important financial concepts, please visit:

www.billkanterpresents.com
www.thetaxfreeplan.com
www.iwanttoretiretaxfree.com
www.doawaywithyour401k.com
www.incomeridervideo.com
www.mediciadalternative.com
www.lazymoneycure.com

About the Author

Bill Kanter is an estate planning attorney and financial planning specialist with over two decades of experience. As the owner of Kanter Wealth Management, LLC, he has served hundreds of clients in the Chicago area to create a financially secure and tax-free future.

Bill earned his J.D and M.B.A from DePaul University College of Law and Graduate School of Business. He lives in Chicago with his wife Valerie and their five children.

If you have questions about your retirement planning, please don't hesitate to contact Bill:

Phone: 847-674-6470
E-mail: bill@kanterwm.com
Website: www.kanterwm.com
Address: 8170 McCormick Blvd., Suite 102, Skokie IL 60076